GHANDL

NINE VISITS TO THE MYTHWORLD

TRANSLATED FROM HAIDA

BY ROBERT BRINGHURST

Masterworks
of the Classical Haida Mythtellers

VOLUME 1
A Story as Sharp as a Knife:
The Classical Haida Mythtellers and Their World

VOLUME 2
Ghandl of the Qayahl Llaanas,
Nine Visits to the Mythworld

VOLUME 3
Skaay of the Qquuna Qiighawaay,
Being in Being

NINE VISITS TO THE MYTHWORLD

Ghandl *of the* Qayahl Llaanas

Translated from Haida
by Robert Bringhurst

2nd edition

Douglas & McIntyre

DOUGLAS AND MCINTYRE (2013) LTD.
P.O. Box 219, Madeira Park
British Columbia, Canada, V0N 2H0
www.douglas-mcintyre.com

Typography: Robert Bringhurst
Printed and bound in Canada · Printed on 100% recycled paper

Douglas and McIntyre acknowledges the support of the Canada Council for the Arts, the Government of Canada, and the Province of British Columbia through the BC Arts Council.

· · · · · · · · ·

Library and Archives Canada Cataloguing in Publication

Title: Nine visits to the mythworld : told by Ghandl of the Qayahl Llaanas / Ghandl of the Qayahl Llaanas ; translated by Robert Bringhurst.
Other titles: Works. Selections. English
Names: Ghandl, author. | Bringhurst, Robert, translator.
Description: Series statement: Masterworks of the classical Haida mythtellers | Includes bibliographical references. | Translated from the original Haida.
Identifiers: Canadiana (print) 20230483585 | Canadiana (ebook) 20230483631 | ISBN 9781771623773 (softcover) | ISBN 9781771623780 (EPUB)
Subjects: LCSH: Haida mythology—British Columbia—Haida Gwaii. | LCSH: Haida poetry—Translations into English. | LCSH: Tales—British Columbia—Haida Gwaii. | CSH: Haida—British Columbia—Haida Gwaii—Folklore.
Classification: LCC E99.H2 G5213 2023 | DDC 398.2089/9728—dc23

· · · · · · · · ·

Cover image: Anonymous Haida artist, *Shaman Diving*. Alder and paint, 59.5 cm high, ca. 1870? (Canadian Museum of History, Gatineau, VII-B-1654).

Contents

As a first approximation, the name *Ghandl* can be pronounced to begin like *gamble* and end like *candle*. To improve on this, move the first consonant, *gh,* down lower in the throat and fuse the *dl* to make a single sound (as in *oddly,* not as in *dull*). Do not introduce a second vowel. *Ghandl* is one syllable (like the *handl* of *handlist*), not two (like *handle* or *Handel*).

Again as a first approximation, *Qayahl* can be pronounced to begin like *kayak* and end like *coral*. To improve on this, pronounce the *q* like *k* but deeper in the throat and make the *hl* a voiceless *l* (tongue in the *l* position while the breath flows tunelessly out from under both sides of the tongue: like *ll* in the Welsh name *Llewelyn*).

Llaanas, as a first approximation, can be pronounced as if composed of the initial syllables in *lanyard* and *aster*. To improve on this, lengthen the first vowel and pronounce the *ll* at the beginning as a glottalized *l* – so that the airflow starts, with a sudden burst, from the glottis, then continues from the lungs.

For a further improvement, go back to the name *Ghandl* and make the *l* at the end voiceless, like the *hl* in *Qayahl*.

For more details of Haida pronunciation, see appendix 2, page 186.

Translator's Acknowledgements

THE POLITICS OF LANGUAGE on the British Columbia coast
are fraught with guilt and anger, ignorance and fear – yet they are also
laced with innocence and wisdom and good will. For the encouragement
and help I have received in making these translations, I am grateful.
This encouragement has come from native speakers of Haida, Cree,
English and Tlingit, and from native speakers of French and Spanish,
Danish, Dutch, German, Italian, Polish and Portuguese. The occasional
flashes of resentment and suspicion prompted by my work with Haida
literature have also been instructive; I am therefore grateful for them
too. It is a fact, however, that all of them have come from persons born
in North America whose native language is English.

These translations – and the larger project of which they are part –
began for me in earnest in 1987, with a fellowship in poetry from the
John Simon Guggenheim Memorial Foundation. I long ago exhausted
the Foundation's monetary gift, but I remain deeply thankful for the
help and the momentum it allowed me to achieve. I am also grateful
to the Canada Council for the Arts, which has supported publication
of this book through its program for literary translation – now happily
enlarged to embrace the literatures of Canada's first nations.

In my attempts to learn my way through the larger panorama of
Native American oral literatures, I have had help from other sources,
largely through the efforts of my colleague Sean Kane. I am grateful in
particular to Thomas H.B. Symons, founding president of Trent University; to Joan Vastokas, former chair of the committee of trustees of
the Symons Trust Fund for Canadian Studies; and to the Social Sciences
and Humanities Research Council of Canada.

I have gained a great deal from discussions with Dell Hymes about the structures of Native American narrative poetry, and from Nancy Turner about Haida ethnobotany. For other helpful comments and suggestions, I am grateful to Ewa Czaykowska-Higgins, Regna Darnell, Gudrun Dreher, Victor Golla, Trevor Goward, Sean Kane, Dennis Lee, Don McKay, Elizabeth McLean, Louise Mercer and Jan Zwicky.

Scott McIntyre played a vital role in the incubation of this book and its two siblings. For his patience and his courage, I remain immensely grateful.

Most of Ghandl's works, it seems to me, are stories about the marriage of people and place. I owe thanks to Trevor Goward and to Valerie Hennell, who permitted me to work on these translations in places they have loved, nurtured and been nurtured by in turn: places whose serenity and beauty they have magnified and maintained.

The introductory volume in this series, *A Story as Sharp as a Knife*, has provoked a number of responses in the year since its release. One of the most detailed of these came from another student of Haida, John Enrico, who listed a large number of instances in which he disagreed with my interpretation of a Haida word or phrase. In half a dozen of these cases, I found that Enrico had indeed spotted errors in my reading, or that I preferred his interpretation to mine, and I have changed my translations accordingly. Only one of these instances affects the translations in this book, and it is mentioned in the endnotes, but I want to extend my thanks to John Enrico for his close attention to my work.

Trevor's Pond · Fête de St Bernard de Montjoux, May 2000

Introduction: *The Blind Poet of Sunshine and Sea Lion Town*

HANDL OF THE QAYAHL LLAANAS was a
Haida-speaking mythteller, born around 1851 in the Haida village
of Qaysun, "Sea Lion Town." It is an empty beachfront now, but
it was home, in the early nineteenth century, to three hundred
people or more, and it was then only one of some forty big villages peppering the thousand-mile coast of an archipelago known
as *Xhaaydla Gwaayaay*. No such places are now listed in offi-
cial gazetteers. Qaysun is an unmarked spot near the northwest
corner of an island known as Moresby, in a cluster of islands
formerly mapped as the Queen Charlottes and now known as
Haida Gwaii, south of the southern tip of Alaska and west of the
British Columbia mainland. On the map and in the tax collector's
ledgers, these islands are a part of Canada, the Commonwealth
of Nations and the continent of North America. Ghandl did not
know or use these names. He knew instead the land, the plants,
the animals of the islands, the speech of his own people, and the
ever-present, ever-changing sea. Qaysun is on the edge of the
continental shelf, facing seven thousand miles of open ocean.

In 1851, the Haida social order was still firmly based on the
matrilineal moiety system. *Moiety* means *half* or *side*. Every Haida
family or lineage[1] belongs to either the Raven side or the Eagle
side. Each member of society is born or adopted into one of these
lineages, and therefore into one of the two sides. Marriage is
sanctioned only between moieties. Slaves and unclassified aliens
therefore stand beyond the pale of traditional social relations.
Ghandl's mother was a member of the Qayahl Llaanas lineage
(the Sea Lion People) of the Eagle side; so therefore were her

children. His father belonged to the Hlghaaxhitgu Llaanas (the Pebble Beach People) of the Raven side.

The first waves of disease brought by visiting Europeans – smallpox, measles, influenza, scarlet fever and other epidemics lethal to millions of Native Americans – had reached the Northwest Coast three-quarters of a century before Ghandl was born, but the worst were yet to come. Within the first five decades of his life, the total Haida population fell from twelve thousand or more to fewer than one thousand. Fully ninety-five per cent of the Haida villages were abandoned. Ghandl survived this holocaust, though not without some scars. Sometime in early manhood, an attack of smallpox or measles cost him his eyesight. From that moment on, he had more time than most of the other survivors to listen to and think about the myths, and fewer ways to make himself of use except by telling them in turn.

When he was in his early thirties, Ghandl left Qaysun and moved, with other survivors, to Xayna Gwaayaay, "Sunshine Island," on the sheltered east side of the archipelago. Here, on an ancient site, a fine new town called Xayna Llanagaay, "Sunshine Village," was optimistically under construction. The houses were built in the latest Haida style, with traditional Haida housepoles but also some modest innovations, such as European doorways and front porches. Here the deaths continued. A few years after Ghandl moved there, Xayna was abandoned in its turn. He and the other survivors moved to the nearby village of Hlghagilda, where a large church had recently been built and an English-speaking preacher was in residence. On the missionary's urging, all the traditional houses in Hlghagilda were demolished and replaced by European-style dwellings; the housepoles, mortuary poles, and most of the memorial poles were removed, and the place, like its people, was given what the missionary thought to be a proper Christian name: Skidegate Mission.

The Haida word *ghandl* (*gandl*) means creek or fresh water. It is likely that Ghandl was given this name as an infant. At Xayna, on 25 December 1887, he acquired another name. A visiting minister christened him Walter McGregor. Many English speakers find the latter name more comfortable to say and to remember.

But Ghandl's work is rooted in indigenous, pre-Christian Haida notions of the world, and he did not speak either English or Scots Gaelic. I feel less disrespectful using Ghandl's Haida name, even knowing that its owner might find fault with my pronunciation.

It was at Hlghagilda (now Skidegate), in November 1900, that Ghandl dictated the texts contained in this book. John Reed Swanton, a linguist, commissioned him to tell these stories and hired another Haida, Henry Moody, to serve as the principal listener. Ghandl dictated, usually six hours a day, six days a week, for roughly three weeks. Moody repeated his words sentence by sentence, hour by hour, and Swanton wrote them down in laborious but usually quite accurate phonetics. Early the next year, Swanton and Moody went over the transcripts word by word to make a literal interlinear translation. Those interlinear translations would be very welcome now, as the best record of just how Henry Moody understood what Ghandl said. But after Swanton used these interlinears, in 1902–3, to make his running prose translation, he apparently destroyed them. What we have to work with now are the Haida texts as Swanton typed them, in Washington, DC, in 1902, and his English prose translations.[2]

➤   ➤   ➤

In some respects, the maturity and character of a work of oral literature depend upon the listener as much as on the teller. It is therefore well worth learning what we can about the people who were there when these dictation sessions occurred. Others probably dropped in from time to time, but three men were there throughout, and each of these was indispensable.

The transcriber, John Swanton, was the youngest. He was 27, remarkably quiet, patient, and well trained for the work he was doing. He had just completed his doctorate in ethnology at Harvard but had done so in absentia, by studying linguistics with Franz Boas at Columbia. He had been in Haida Gwaii for five weeks when he began to work with Ghandl, and he stayed nearly a year, funded by the Bureau of American Ethnology in Washington, DC, and the American Museum of Natural History in New York. Swanton had studied the Haida language day in and day out since arriving in the Islands, but in November 1900, he cannot have understood more than a part of what Ghandl was saying. Yet because of his patience and his training, he was able to transcribe the stories well.

Henry Moody, the principal listener, was roughly 30. He was adaptable and modern enough to be active in the church and impressively bilingual, yet traditional enough to have listened to and thought about a lot of Haida mythology, and he was handsomely connected with the village aristocracy that led the old regime. Through his mother, he was heir to his uncle Gidansta, headman of Qquuna, a large village south of Hlghagilda. His father was Gumsiiwa, headman of the village of Hlqiinul. By 1900 Qquuna and Hlqiinul both stood empty, like Qaysun, yet their prestige had not been lost. So Henry Moody was entitled by his rank, as well as by his age and personal demeanor, to hear Ghandl's most sophisticated work. The listener was linked to the teller by bonds beyond the tradition as well. One was sighted; one was blind; but both men were survivors – and colonial encroachment had made both men refugees in their own land.

Ghandl himself, when he dictated these stories, was probably 49.[3] This is young for a mythteller, and not every work that he performed for Moody and Swanton seems, in retrospect, fully matured. But Swanton asked for every story Ghandl was willing to tell, and asked especially for stories he could not hear elsewhere – stories linked to the depeopled west coast, and stories Ghandl might have heard that had belonged to other families whose master storytellers had died. Ghandl's weaker stories (there are four of these in total, in my judgment – three of which are really only summaries of stories) appear to have been told in response to such requests.[4]

The nine stories in this book are those I believe to be his best. Each is a subtly constructed, vibrant reenvisioning of a myth that both illuminates and enlightens. Each embodies Ghandl's sense of the numinous liveliness of the world and his acute awareness of the hues of human character. Each is intricate enough that it may baffle and surprise when first encountered; but listened to with care, each one casts its light both outward and within.

While these nine stories show Ghandl's many talents as a mythteller, they do not reveal the full scope of his work with Swanton and Moody. Two substantial works not included in this book, along with fragments in Swanton's two surviving notebooks, add something to the picture. Ghandl's skills as a composer of explanatory and analytical narrative are clear from a long piece he dictated, at Swanton's request, to clarify the workings of a major Haida social institution, the *waahlgal*. This is one of the two main types of Haida potlatch or celebratory feast. Ghandl's dissertation on this subject was improvised to meet a very unusual state of affairs. It was not, in 1900, common practice for interested, intelligent but ignorant outsiders to ask detailed questions about Haida institutions. Yet Ghandl's answer is as lucid and as formal in its way as his performances of the myths.[5] His skill with a third genre, mythic burlesque, is also clear from his performance of "The Youngsters' Tale," presented as a complement and sequel to "The Elders' Tale" as performed by his older colleague Skaay.[6] These terms are worth a moment's investigation.

The Elders' Tale and the Youngsters' Tale are the two principal components found in classical Haida performances of the myth cycle known as *Raven Travelling*. Both components take the form of spoken narrative, but perhaps the simplest way to distinguish one from another is by means of some theatrical and musical analogies. The Elders' Tale is a kind of scandalous, hilarious yet eminently serious tragicomic drama. It reveals, through the agency of the Raven, how the world came to be as perfectly imperfect as it is. The Youngsters' Tale is something like the corresponding satyr play, performed on its own as entertainment or with the Elders' Tale as a kind of comic warm-up act or encore.

The Youngsters' Tale is also not so much a tale as a chain of little tales, an anthology of short comic episodes explaining any number of phenomena – biological, geological or social – through the actions of the trickster. Elders' Tale and Youngsters' Tale can overlap extensively in content and in tone, but they differ fundamentally in structure. Well-made versions of the Elders' Tale take a larger view and have an overarching shape, like a sonata. The Youngsters' Tale is more like theme and variations. Or to

13

speak in terms of film, the Elders' Tale is the main feature; the Youngsters' Tale is a thematically connected cycle of cartoons. There are structures in everybody's stories, as in everybody's sentences. But one thing that distinguishes a real oral poet from a raconteur or gossip is how those structures shine and resonate and sing. In each of the nine stories in this book, the structure does all that. These, in other words, are something more than comic entertainments and were not composed for children.

Tradition is important in Native American cultures, as it is in every functioning culture, but the major works of Native American literature are major works of art, and the makers of these works are every bit as individual as any artists anywhere. It seems to me quite wrong to describe such works as "folklore" or as "Indian legends." They are never, at root, anonymous. Nor are they works of corporate authorship, mindlessly recited by nameless, faceless agents of the tribe. If Ghandl's poems are folk tales, then the paintings of Andrea Mantegna are folk art and the sonatas of Franz Schubert are folk music. None of these works could come to be without the force of a living tradition, but none of them is the fruit of tradition alone.

Erna Gunther, a respected and respectful anthropologist, worked for many years among the Coast Salish peoples of Puget Sound, a thousand miles south of Haida Gwaii. In 1925, she published *Klallam Tales*, an anthology of stories told to her in the Klallam language – but the stories were interpreted on the spot by a multilingual colleague and written down in English only. Gunther makes a point of naming the narrator of each story, but she did not record, as Swanton did, any narrator's actual words. Gunther presupposed – correctly, I am sure – that stories told by Klallam individuals could give her a kind of insight into the mind of the Klallam nation as a whole. But I am puzzled by another of her assumptions – one widely shared by anthropologists at work in the 1920s and shared by some in the present day. Gunther says in the introduction to her book that "One of the problems in the study of oral literature is the influence of the narrator on the literary style of the story."[7]

I imagine that by reading French or Russian novels I can learn quite a bit about the mind of the French or Russian nation. It would not, however, usually occur to me to say that one of the *problems* in the study of written literature is the *writer's* influence on the style. The effect of the narrator on the story is a problem in the same sense that the hinges are a problem for the door.

Are individuals in cultures that are literate always predisposed to undervalue those in cultures that are oral? I do not know. I know however that the habit can be broken and the prejudice unlearned. Jeremiah Curtin, who died in 1906, was one of the earliest outsiders to make a serious study of Native American oral literature. Curtin understood quite well the vital role of individual creativity in the work of the Seneca, Wintu, Yana and Kiksht-speaking mythtellers he knew. Edward Sapir, who began serious work with Native American texts in the same year Curtin died, registered his own enlightenment on this point a few years later, in a tribute to Saayaach'apis, his old Nuuchahnulth teacher. Melville Jacobs made a similar discovery working with Sahaptin, Kiksht, Hanis, and Miluk speakers in the 1920s and early 1930s. Other writers have experienced equivalent revelations through contact with other oral cultures elsewhere in the world. Marcel Griaule's account of what he learned in Africa in 1946 from his Dogon tutor Ogotemmêli, and Victor Turner's vivid portrait of Muchona, his Ndembu teacher, are two notable examples.[8]

Ghandl is not here now to show us all, in person, how an individual talent interacts with the tradition in an oral culture, but it is also possible to learn this lesson less directly, through the study and comparison of artifacts or texts. Bill Reid, who taught me much of what I know of Haida art, was intensely aware of the identities of carvers who had died before he was born. He knew the older masters through their works, although he never knew their names. Dell Hymes's detailed studies of Native American texts, conducted over nearly half a century, point strongly in the same direction.[9] When we study Native American art *as art* and Native American oral literature *as literature,* this is where we head. We learn that the insights and the styles of individual human beings are essential to the symbiotic life of the tradition. Then we can accept them as a treasure, not a problem.

That spark of recognition is dimmed, if not extinguished, where the works are not transcribed in the mythteller's actual language. The major literary works in nearly every Native American language are now apparently condemned to a life lived mostly in translation. But translation that is too quick and easy strips the other's otherness away. And when you take the other's otherness away, the other's sameness and humanity go too.

Like Shakespeare's plays or Rembrandt's paintings, Ghandl's poems reach far beyond the world in which their maker lived, yet they never lose their touch with the environment he knew. His story of "Someone Just About to Go Out Hunting Birds" addresses a theme – the Swan Maiden theme – that is nearly global in distribution. Ghandl makes the story quintessentially Haida at the same time that he makes it his alone. He roots it in the heart and in the ground that is his home. That is how he makes it human, and thereby universally germane.

"A Red Feather" is set in the Nisga'a village of Kwunwoq and deals with a theme well known to Nisga'a people and their neighbours the Gitxsan. Indeed, it is a theme some Gitxsan and Nisga'a now regard as their exclusive cultural property.[10] But Ghandl treats the story as a myth, which is a richly complex piece of knowledge, like a theorem or a language or a genome: an inheritance too precious to be left, like a trademark or a patented procedure, in the realm of the privately owned.

His longest extant work, "Hlagwajiina and His Family," is full of foreign names. It begins in Tlingit country and eventually moves inland to the country of the Tahltan, never touching Haida Gwaii. Yet it too proves to be a mirror of Haida concerns, and of human concerns – in the same way that a play set in Denmark or in Rome can prove a vessel of ideas for those who live their lives in England – and in many other corners of the world. One of Ghandl's younger, bilingual Haida contemporaries, a man by the name of Kihlguulins (Henry Edenshaw), who later became one of Swanton's friends and teachers, developed a great passion for Shakespeare. If the future of the language had looked brighter in his time, he might have felt it worth his while to translate Shakespeare into Haida.

> ▸　　　▸　　　▸

All but one of the stories in this book belong to the genre known in Haida as *k̲'aygaang*. This is to say, they are narrative poems set in mythtime. They are stories in which mythtime rises like a tide and covers, for a timeless moment, a familiar human space. The exception is "The Names of Their Gambling Sticks." This is a *k̲'ayaagaang*, a story in which mythtime coexists with historical time. The *k̲'ayaagaang* are family stories, authenticating the privileges and claims of Haida lineages by linking them to visionary space, where mythtime perseveres.[11]

Mythtime is wild time; historical time is domesticated time. Ghandl, as a trained and skillful mythteller, is well acquainted with both. He also knows that mythtime surrounds historical time, much the way the forest and the ocean and the sky surround the village or the camp. *Wild* does not, of course, mean *disordered*. It means *ecologically ordered*: self-sustaining, alive and quite independent of human control.

In "The Names of Their Gambling Sticks," a human who lives in historical time ventures into the world of myth and vision, then returns, enriched, to his village, much as we do after we have dreamed or told or listened to a myth. But here the reaching out and the returning to domesticated time occur *within the confines of the story*. This is what shifts the story to a different literary genre. The *k̲'ayaagaang* are also used for different purposes than *k̲'aygaang*. They establish claims to lands and other resources, and to names, heraldic crests, songs and other ritual privileges and procedures. It is for this very practical reason that the genre distinction persists.

K̲'ayaagaang and *k̲'aygaang* alike affirm that the boundary between the historical and the mythic, the domestic and the wild, is a flexible and permeable boundary, risky but not difficult to cross, and that the wild, *because* it is not under human control, is not only a dangerous realm but also a source of rebirth: a place to renew and increase one's share of knowledge and power.

Unlike most *k'ayaagaang*, "The Names of Their Gambling Sticks" ratifies a link between two lineages and authenticates privileges of each. The protagonist is a young man of the Jaxwi Sqwaahladagaay (the Seaward Paddlers) of the Raven side.[12] In the course of the story, he acquires prowess as a gambler, confirmed by a new set of names for his gambling sticks, and is rewarded by his father with a new heraldic tattoo. The young man has a gift for his father as well: a new name for his house, which will serve as the occasion for raising a new pole. Ghandl does not say so, but the father in this story has to be of his own lineage, the Qayahl Llaanas. The housename mentioned in the story, *Na Kaaji Stins*, "Two-Headed House," is Qayahl Llaanas property. A Qayahl Llaanas headman built a house of that name at Qaysun, and it may well have been the house where Ghandl lived as a young man. Just beneath the double head are the figures of the Eagle and the Humpback Whale, who are central to "The Myth of the One Who Got Rid of Nine of His Nephews."

Another of these stories, "The Sea Lion Hunter," hovers near the border between *k'aygaang* and *k'ayaagaang*, though it does not slip across. It consists of three main themes, interlocking like the figures on a well-made Haida pole. First is the theme of the sea lion hunter abandoned by his fellows, who is taken beneath the sea to visit the sea lions, tested by them, then helped to return to the human realm. Second is the theme of the carver who creates, from blocks of wood, several species of cetaceans, including killer whales. Third is the theme of a hunter who kills and skins a creature called the *Waasgu* or Seawolf, then secretly goes hunting in its skin and uses his catch to entrap an arrogant mother-in-law who has treated him with disdain. All three themes are widely known and told on the Northwest Coast, and every skilled mythteller handles them differently. Many artists join the first two themes, but of all the classical mythtellers on record in all the coastal languages, only Ghandl integrates all three. He also gives the story a singular ending:

Wasgwaay k̲'al ising agang giiguyingasi.
Gyaan kunaay angga gut̲ga 'la isdaasi
gyaan gam nang 'la k̲'iitl'x̲ahlgansi.

page 96: lines 308–313

Kunaay sk̲aw 'l gingitl'x̲iidagyaalang wansuuga.
'L k̲yaaga dawganaagas gan
    'la waahlgal tlaalang wansuuga.
'La 'la giidaadas.

The Seawolf skin swam out to sea alone.
Then the hunter took the string of whales
and said that no one was to touch them.

The sale of those whales made him rich, they say.
And then he held ten feasts in honor, so they say,
*   of the youngest brother of his wife.*
He made a prince of him.

It is this mention of potlatch and prestige in the conclusion that gives the story something of the flavor of k̲'ayaagaang.[13] This is unlikely to be accidental. We are, after all, hearing a man of the Sea Lion lineage, born in a village called Sea Lion Town, recounting the adventures of a man who has acquired extraordinary powers through a privileged relationship with sea lions. Still, no claim to special rights is made on behalf of the hunter's lineage, nor would such a claim make sense in the context of this ending. The hunter names as his beneficiary not his sister's son (who would be of his own lineage) but the brother of his wife (who necessarily belongs to the opposite side). Here as in "The Names of Their Gambling Sticks," reciprocity is one of the key themes, but the logic of the story is internal, not external. It ends the way it does because of something that occurs *within* the story, not in order to account for social practices outside.

Like a carver adzing out the forms, Ghandl chips away expertly at the tale. Stroke by stroke, clause by clause, image by image it builds. Carver and poet alike leave as the sign of their craftsmanship a lively, patterned surface, as distinctive as a fingerprint. The clauses form sentences, the sentences form clusters, which we might call stanzas, and the clusters form still larger constellations. We can call the larger units *scenes*, by analogy with drama, or *sections*, by analogy with music. In a story of any size, these form larger units in their turn, which we might call *acts* or *movements*. More often than not in Haida oral literature there are five such movements in a story. As a rule there are five (less often three, and still less often ten) sections in a movement, and five (less often three) subsections in a section.

Purely for convenience, I have numbered all the movements (acts) in each of Ghandl's poems. In the longer movements, I have also numbered the sections (scenes). This rudimentary analysis could be carried to a much finer level of detail. If it were, it would have a further impact on the typographic layout of the poems.

Again for mere convenience, I have numbered all the lines. These lines are primarily units of thought (as lines routinely are in what is called *free verse*) and only secondarily units of sound (as lines routinely are in *metered* verse). Here, however, the line isn't quite so arbitrarily defined as it usually is in modern poetry. A line in these translations is essentially a clause. The number of lines in a given passage therefore coincides, more often than not, with the number of verbs in the original (though one Haida verb may become two or three in English translation). In theory this is ludicrously simple; in practice it is less so. If the structural analysis went further, the top-down division into progressively smaller thematic units and the bottom-up division into lines and groups of lines would correct one another and then fuse.

It seems to me that a close reading of any of these stories requires some degree of structural analysis, just as learning to perform a piece of music requires the performer to come to some decisions about how the piece is built. A thoroughgoing structural analysis is a separate undertaking – one that on occasion leaves the pleasures of the music or the literature behind. I find the patterns in Ghandl's stories a constant source of delight, but my analyses remain incomplete in every case.

Over the last forty years, a number of researchers, notably Dell and Virginia Hymes, have studied such patterns in detail and have shown that structures of this kind are a prominent feature of oral narrative all around the world. The particular patterns vary from culture to culture and of course can be employed in different ways, with greater or lesser artistry, by different individuals – but the fact of narrative patterning is no less universal than other linguistic phenomena such as the noun, the verb, the morpheme and the sentence. There is nothing whatever remarkable in the fact that Ghandl's narratives are patterned nor in the fact that they routinely have five movements. This is normal for a Haida story – as it is for an Elizabethan play, whether well or poorly made, to have five acts, and for a foot to have five toes (or four or three or two or one, depending on the genus). Ghandl's stories are remarkable in *how these structures are employed*: how the movements and the sections fit together; how the structures, whether simple or complex, stand up and dance.

The patterns are *fractal* in the sense that they repeat at varying scales. It may also be the case that, like many fractal structures found in nature, they cause the story to behave like something larger than it looks.[14] They are, it seems to me, something like the nervous system of the story. Branching and rebranching as they do, they multiply the story's information-bearing capacity, and I suspect that, as it travels from one teller to the next, they encourage and restrain its evolution and mutation. It is not, then, entirely surprising that representing them on the page can also add to the information-bearing capacity of the printed text. But what kind of added information do we get?

Joan Tenenbaum and Mary Jane McGary are among the few scholars who have published the same set of oral texts in both the smooth typography of prose and in the imbricated form that we associate with verse. McGary explains why they switched from the former to the latter in re-editing the works of Antone Evan and other Tanaina storytellers from southern Alaska:

The line and stanza format merely makes it possible to include more information about the way the stories were told than a plain prose presentation would. It also seems to make reading the stories more like hearing them, perhaps because we read verse lines more slowly and with more concentration than we read blocks of prose.[15]

Tenenbaum and McGary were dealing with texts that had been taped before they were transcribed. They therefore had the option of basing their typography wholly or in part on surface features of performance. Most of the classical literature that survives in Native American languages (and all that survives in classical Haida) was transcribed from live dictation. In the absence of an audio recording, reconstructing the original performance, even in an abstract, typographic form, is far beyond our reach. What we can try to reconstruct is the performable deep structure of the story. It is no less feasible to do this than it is to reconstruct the metrical shape of Pindar's poems in classical Greek, when all we have to work with are papyri where the verse has been written out as prose. But uncovering a structure implicit in the text and faithfully portraying a particular performance are never quite the same. Working out the structure and the phrasing in a piece for strings or keyboard is likewise not the same as working out the fingering that will give the desired result.[16]

There is of course a tendency in all human speech for units of thought and units of sound to coincide.[17] Part of the pleasure of hearing and understanding any language – verse, prose or anything else, including the verbal plasma of conversation – comes in sensing how the thought-shapes and sound-shapes go in and out of phase. Even in and of themselves, the shapes of thought and sound in language are complex; they have their own subcomponents that go in and out of phase. Behind them is the shifting cantus firmus of the breath, with which the rhythms and the shapes of thought and sound tend again to coincide – but always with delicious imperfection. No form of typographic notation can represent the web of language fully. If it did, such a wealth of information would suffocate us all. Even after they have moved from the oral world to the world of writing, myth and music need some room in which to breathe. We have to re-create these stories as we read. Anything more passive is a form of disrespect to Ghandl and the culture he inherited.

So the purpose of the typographic form is to reveal an order that is there, implicit in the text, and thus to give more information – but not to give too much of it up front. It is to give the information without using up the breathing room it needs.

➤   ➤   ➤

There is more, I think, to be learned from the metaphor of the adze. Haida carvers routinely use the adze to make both forms and surface patterns. These contain the signature of the human species, the signature of the culture and the signature of the individual carver. So do the patterns formed by the mythteller's sentences. Mimicking these patterns perfectly in English is beyond me. There is only a small overlap between the repertoire of forms for an English sentence and the repertoire of forms for a sentence in Haida. Still, a clause is a clause, and a sentence is a sentence. In the patterns formed by groups of sentences and clauses, the translation and the text can more closely coincide.

We can call these clusters of clauses and sentences *stanzas* or *verse paragraphs,* but neither of these names suggests the logical syntax or *patterned movement of thought* by which the clusters are defined. Each small cluster of sentences fulfills, in its singular way, an established noetic pattern, just as each of Sappho's lines fulfills anew a familiar metrical pattern, and each of Joyce's sentences fulfills anew an old syntactic form. In the hands of a skilled mythteller, each fulfillment of such a pattern is a delight in itself; at the same time, it advances the dance of the story. In short, this is poetry in which the *prosody of meaning* is usually stronger than the prosody of sound. Each cluster of sentences constitutes, in effect, a *narrative syllogism.*

This is a very simple example, from the story of the shaman known as *Stl'uughut Sghaanaghwaay* or "Spirit Being Living in the Little Finger":

page 44:
lines
76–78

'L iijaas gangaaxan
ising 'la iijagaay dluu
ll gyaaxatl'xas.

After doing once more
what he'd already done,
he suddenly stood up.

This could, of course, be said in other ways, but this is how to
say it taking three crisp steps, instead of one or two that might
be less crisp. The result is a syllogistic form: a tiny shard of narrative as precise in its way as a snowflake or a geometric proof
or a logical deduction. It is also a tiny piece of conceptual music:
three simple statements forming in the silence of the mind an
arpeggiated chord: a tiny but shapely and resonant piece of the
action.

There are two- and four- and five-part syllogisms too. On the
page they look like two- and four- and five-line stanzas or verse
paragraphs. In the mind they act like two- and four- and five-
note chords in which the notes are nouns and verbs. The simple
triad seems to me the most basic of these syllogistic forms, and
in Haida it is one of the most common. Another very common
form of Haida narrative syllogism involves five steps, often sub-
divided into three plus two. The steps may also be more complex
than they are in the previous example. This is such a syllogism,
taken from the same story:

pp 51–52:
lines
282–286

'L k'utl'uu stahlastansingaay dluu
xilaay kungastagang 'la ts'ingulgadangaay dluu
'laga lla kaagang wansuuga.
Kiidangwaay at 'la 'la kiijiyaay dluu
'l xiihlaga ll dldasdyas.

When it had spouted four times
and he had spat the medicine ahead of him,
he went to it, they say.

After he had snagged it with the gaffhook,
he found himself in its mouth.

It would be possible, I think, to count and name the forms
of syllogism used in Haida narrative, just as it is in Aristotelian
logic. They might turn out to be as deceptively few and simple
as the elemental forms in Haida formline painting.[18] But in logic
and in painting and in narrative alike, it is not so much the forms
that seem to matter. It is how the forms are used. The narrative
syllogism in Haida can be used to say something dull, something
pedantic, or something that can take your mental breath away
and give it back, transformed.

The fact that they can do this is what makes it irresistible, to
me, to speak of Ghandl's narratives as poems.

⸳   ⸳   ⸳

Bonus dormitat Homerus, Horace says.[19] "Good Homer dozes off"
– and so does every oral poet, old and new. Homer comes to us,
however, through two and a half millennia of patient editorial
repair and conservation as well as the explication, repetition and
popularization that make the oral narratives of Greece appear
deceptively complete and easy to digest. Ghandl, who belongs to
a tradition just as old, does not come wrapped in the same cloud
of illusory security. Because his voice is fresh, it may at first seem
raw, but its subtleties will show themselves in time to anyone
who listens – even those who listen only with their eyes. Along
with the inevitable, minor slipped stitches in the poems, there
is-overwhelming evidence of powerful, graceful and pervasive
intellectual and emotional organization. And gestures that may
look at first like slips – such as failing to complete a standard list
or set of repetitions – turn out to be not slips but skilled elisions.
They are gestures of the kind that we expect performing artists –
concert pianists for instance – to make as and when they please.

In North American society over the past forty years, a slow shift
has occurred in the treatment accorded to works by indigenous
visual artists, both living and dead. Institutions and historians

have grown in general less content to accept such works of art as anonymous creations and more determined to establish their real authorship.[20] It is the barrier of language, I suppose, which explains why literary scholars and institutions have lagged so far behind the art historians and museums.

Language is no less essential to literature than muscles to the dance or substance to a sculpture, and yet there comes a point at which all such material embodiments, essential though they are, can also be impediments. There comes a point at which the substance has to let the vision go the extra disembodied inch. It seems to me this only happens when the vision is propelled through someone's solitary, singular and overwhelming wish. I think it happens in these poems. That, I think, is what entitles us to speak of Ghandl's work in much the way that Bill Reid spoke half a century ago about a certain unassuming little piece of Haida sculpture:

It's silly to say this shaman's rattle has got to be one of the great pieces of Northwest Coast art.... But we could go on forever saying the same thing. It's not just great Northwest Coast art, what the hell, it's one of the greatest examples of human expression.

We have to see into the mind behind this piece.... He [the artist] had a problem. He thought it through and obviously drew on all levels of his consciousness to bring this to fruition. He did it and it worked. He took it to the person who had commissioned it, and I suppose the joy of that ... creation eventually permeated the entire society; and now, if you want to get high-flown about it, it enhances the whole human experience by its existence. It's the other side of the human coin from the obvious, the trite.[21]

NINE VISITS

TO THE MYTHWORLD

[···] square brackets mark editorial restorations
⟨ ··· ⟩ angle brackets mark editorial insertions

The Way the Weather
Chose to Be Born[1]

T HERE WAS A CHILD OF GOOD FAMILY, they say, [1]
at Swiftcurrent Creek.[2]
And her father had one of his slaves constantly watching her.
She said to the slave,
«Tell that one I want to make love to him.»

The day after that, when she went
       out of doors with the slave,
she asked if he'd said
what she told him to say.

And the slave said to the young woman,
«He says he's afraid of your father.»   10
But the slave had spoken to no one.
The slave was in love with her, they say.

When she had decided on somebody else,
she gave the slave the same instructions.
He failed again to deliver the message.
He told her again
that the man was afraid of her father.

After sending the message to each of her father's ten nephews,
the one of good family made love with the slave, they say.
And her father found out it had happened.   20

So they all moved away from her, they say.
And no one but her youngest uncle's wife
    left food for her, they say.

S HE WENT digging for shellfish, they say.   [2.1]
  After a while, she dug up a cockleshell.
The cry of a child came from inside it.

She looked at it closely.
The embryo of a child was living inside it.
She carried it into the house.
She put birds' down around it.

Then, though she gave it no milk,   30
it grew very quickly.
Soon it started crawling
Soon after that it was walking.

O NE DAY the child said,   [2.2]
  «Mother, like this.»
He was gesturing with his hands.
When he did it again,
she knew what he wanted.

She hammered a copper bracelet into a bow.
She hammered another one into an arrow.   40
After she finished a second arrow,
she gave him the weapons.
Then he was happy.

And then he went hunting for birds.
He came back with a cormorant for his mother.
She ate it.

The next day again he went hunting for birds,
and he brought in a goose for his mother, they say.

32

She ate it.

The next day again he went hunting for birds.   50
He brought in a wren.
He skinned it himself,
and he dried the skin.
He cherished it.

Next day, he brought in a song sparrow.
This too he skinned by himself,
and he dried the skin.

The next day he brought in a Steller's jay,
and he skinned it
and dried it.   60

The day after that, he brought in a redheaded sapsucker.
He skinned it as well,
and he dried it.

T HEN in the night something spoke to his mother.   [2.3]
     Just at that moment, the house started creaking.
Next morning he woke in a well-finished building.
The carvings on the houseposts winked their eyes.
Master Carver had adopted him, they say.

He got up.
And his father said to him,   70
«Well, my young lord, let me paint you.»

He went to his father.
His father put level streaks of cloud on his face.
«Now, my young lord, sit facing the sea.»
And the moment he did so, the weather was fine.

T HEN ONE DAY he asked his father   [3]
    to come with him on a fishing trip, they say.
«We're going to catch the fish-catching octopus.»[3]
And he fished for it and he caught it.

They drifted with the current over House Banks.
He told his father to sit in the bow.   80
He looked at the rising sun for a while.

Then he said, «Father, say this:
The Largest One of Them All is thinking of biting.»
His father said these very words.

«Father, say this:
  *The One Who Travels All around the Islands
          is thinking of biting.*»
And he spoke these very words.

«Father, say *Sir, shadows are falling on Steep Rock Mountain.
  Make up your mind.*»
And he spoke these very words.   90

«Father, say this:
  *The Big One Who Comes to Swiftcurrent Creek
          is thinking of biting.*»
And he said those very words.

«Father, say this:
  The Big One Slurping Up Pebbles is thinking of biting.»
He said it.

And then, «Father, say this:
  The One with White Stone Eyes has looked it over.»

«Father, say this:

The Big One Who Feeds Wherever He Pleases
    is thinking of biting.»   100
He said these very words.

As soon as he had said these things,
it took the bait, they say.
And then it towed them right around the Islands.

He slapped the canoe on the gunwales, they say.
And he said to it,
«Master Carver made you.
Swim with your head up.»
Then it towed them round the Islands once again.

When they came to rest,   110
he hauled in the line.
And he brought to the surface the face
      of something amazing.

A forest of broad-bladed kelp surrounded its mouth.
There were halibut nesting all over it.
Then, they say, he started to bring them aboard.

He filled his canoe.
Then he stretched it out larger.
He kept on hauling them aboard,
and he again filled his canoe.
Then they released it.   120

They paddled back to town in their canoe.
Master Carver brought the halibut up to his wife.
She cut it and dried it.

Then he called his son once more, they say.
And after he had painted him, he said,
«My son, your uncles are living in that direction.

Go there and see.»
And he went there, they say.

At the edge of the town, he sat down.
When he had sat there awhile, they saw him.   130
They crowded around him.

They knew him at once, they say.
And then they moved back where his mother was living.

WHEN all of them had lived there for a while,   [4.1]
he went out of the house
        dressed in his wren skin, they say.
«Come look at me, mother,» he said.
And his mother followed him outside.
She saw him poised above the sea as a cumulus cloud.

Then they came in,
and he said to his mother,   140
«Did I look handsome?»
«Yes, my young lord, you looked fine.»

Next, they say, he went out in the skin of the Steller's jay.
And he said to his mother,
«Come look at me.»
She followed him outside.
Above the sea, her son was spread out wide and blue.

Then they came in,
and he said, «Did I look handsome, mother?»
«Yes, my young lord, you looked fine.»   150

Then he went out in his sapsucker skin.
And he said, «Come look at me, mother.»
His mother followed him outside.
He was bright red high above the sea.[4]

She smiled at her son.
When they came back in, he said,
«Did I look handsome, mother?»
«Yes, my young lord.
The spirit-beings will never grow tired of seeing your face.»

«This is the last I will see of you, mother,» he said.   160
«I am going away.
Whenever I sit where the Tallgrass River reaches the sea,
no wind will blow from any direction.
The sky will be mine.

«Whenever my face is the same as my father painted it,
no wind will blow from any direction.
Humans will feed themselves through me.»

«Very well, my young lord.
Whenever you sit there,
I will scatter feathers in your honor.»   170

T HEN he left his mother, they say.   [4.2]
    And his father got ready to leave her as well.

«I also am going away,» he said.
«Make your home at the headwaters.
I will be watching for you there,
and I will also be watching for my son.»
Then he left her there, they say.

A S THE DAY was ending,   [4.3]
    she called her youngest uncle aside.
«Tomorrow,» she said, «when you and your brothers
            go fishing,   180
    wear a new hat
    and take a new paddle.»

And early next day, they all went out fishing.
She sat at the end of the town
and stretched out her legs.
When she pulled up her skirt,
the wind blew out of the inlet.

The higher she raised it, the fiercer the wind.
When her skirt came up over her knees,
a gale was blowing.   190

And she clung to the thread
of the one who wore a new hat.
She saved him, they say, and him only,
because of his wife, who had left her some food.
She is Fairweather Woman, they say.

THEN she went inland, they say,   [5]
taking her mats and all her belongings.
She walked up the bed of the creek,
and she settled there.

Later a trail was cut over top of her.   200
The traffic disturbed her, she said,
and she moved farther inland.
She sank to her buttocks, they say.
There, they say, she is one with the ground.

When her son takes his place,
she scatters flakes of snow for him.
Those are the feathers.

That is the end.   208

Spirit Being
Living in the Little Finger[1]

I N THE TOWN OF WHITE HILLSIDE,[2] they say,   [1.1]
    they turned against a mother and her child.

The child built a brushwood shelter at the end of town
for both of them to live in.
He walked the beach at each low tide
and brought his mother
what he found in the way of food.

After he'd been doing this awhile,
he met a great blue heron with a broken beak.
The boy made it sharp again.

«Grandson,» said the heron,   10
«you have helped me.
I will help you too.
Now chew these leaves.»

The second thing he gave him
    was a feather from his wingtip, saying,
«Use your breath to send this feather underneath the arm
    of the favoured child of the town.
Even the spirit beings will not perceive it.»

T HE BOY played at being a shaman, they say.   [1.2]
  He made a dancing apron out of a mat.

He fastened periwinkle shells around the fringe
and made a periwinkle rattle.   20
He danced wearing feathers that he found.
He used a cedarbark basket for a drum.

That evening, he walked through the town.
He looked through a fissure in the wall
          of the largest of the houses.
The child of good family sat inside.

He pushed the feather in between the houseplanks.
When it pointed toward the armpit,
he exhaled.

Instantly the feather went beneath his arm,
and the child of good family was in anguish.   30
Then this one walked away.

THEY SENT for a shaman.   [1.3]
    This one tagged along
to watch him dance, they say.

Little darkskinned people stood inside the door
with pitchwood torches.
Then he thought,
«Can't they see it sticking out of him?»

One of the doormen set his torch aside,
and chased him out, they say.
He ran away.   40
That was The One Who Has Spines in His Ears, they say.

He went again on the following day.
He followed the shaman in.
When the same thought crossed his mind,
the same one chased him out again, they say.

Then, they say, they knew it was the boy.
And then they came to him in a crowd.

HE CHEWED the medicine and spat it on the things   [1.4]
   he had been playing with.
On the dancing apron suddenly a painted face appeared.   50
On the drum there was the image of the Seawolf.[3]
The dancing hat was decorated too.

Then they hung five moosehides up to pay him,
and he went there.
The plank drum and beating sticks came through the door
     by themselves, beating time.
His own drum came in drumming itself too.

They propped the door wide open in his honor with a pole.
While they watched for him there in the doorway,
his dancing hat entered the house by itself
     through the opposite wall, they say,
         from in back of the fire.

Then it did it again from one side of the house,   60
and again from the front
and again from one side.
When his hat had hovered in four directions,
he stood there.

He reached for the feather.
Then he withdrew it.
He drew in his breath so the feather's tip was exposed,
and the pain disappeared.

Just before he went out of the house,
he breathed it back in again.   70
He refused what they offered him.
Then he went off.

O<small>N THE FOLLOWING DAY,</small> they hung   [1.5]
     ten moosehides up
and he came to them again.
His own drum and the plank drum
     went through the door again by themselves.

After doing once more
what he'd already done,
he suddenly stood up.

Letting his dancing hat float in mid-air for a while,
he pulled out the feather completely.   80
Then the child of good family fell asleep.

        ➤   ➤   ➤

H<small>E HAD</small> many uncles who started suggesting   [2.1]
     he marry their daughters.
Another had a daughter who was withered on one side.
That was his youngest uncle's daughter, they say.

Once, when the people were planning to go on an outing,
he left the town ahead of them, they say.
He took on the form of a salmonberry bush beside the trail.
He waited there, they say.

When the girl with the withered side came by,   90
he tangled himself in her hair.
While she tried to get free,
the others kept walking.

Then he came out and stood next to her.
«You are the one I will marry,» he said to her.
«Come with me.»
And she went with him, they say.

44

W HEN she entered the house with him,   [2.2]
      he chewed the medicine and lathered it over her body.
He stretched out her leg.   100
She grew healthy and whole.
Then he made love to her.

And then he tore the brushwood shelter down
and built himself a house.
He screened off a space for himself
and he slept there with his wife.

H E WOKE in the night   [2.3]
      as the house moved under him, they say.
He heard someone speaking with his mother.

When daylight came,   110
and he opened his eyes,
he found himself surrounded by something amazing.
The carvings on the houseposts winked their eyes.
The carvings on the bedframe flicked their tongues.

In one of the back corners of the house,
            something stood and shook like thunder.
It was Stickwalking God, they say.
Master Carver, they say, had made himself into his father.

When he stepped out of bed,
Master Carver called him over.
«My son, let me make you presentable.»   120

This one went up to him then,
and that one combed his hair.
It hung down clean and shining to his hips.
He painted this one's face as well.
He made him good looking, they say.

                    ⸲   ⸲   ⸲

Once he had lived in the house with his father awhile,　[3.1]
　　he decided to marry the daughter of Rockfacet Cliff.
His father had told him .
that Rockfacet Cliff was destroying those who are
　　　　spirit beings from birth.

And his father gave him the arrows he needed, they say.　　130
«They fly everywhere together,»
said his father.
On one was the figure of a weasel.
On the other was the figure of a mouse.

His father also gave him knots and burls from dry trees.
«In his village, driftwood never floats ashore,»
his father said.
And his father sent Stickwalking God
to make certain he got there.

After they had travelled for a ways,　　　　　　　　　140
he saw that the points of land they were passing
were burning.
This one spat his medicine across them
and that one vaulted over them on his pole.

When they passed close to Maghan,[4]
something tasted good to him.
Beach potatoes[5] grow there in profusion.
That's what made him feel that way, they say.

Once he had brought him to one end of Rockfacet's village,
Stickwalking God went back
　　where he'd come from, they say.　　　　　　　　　150

When evening fell,　　　　　　　　　　　　　　　[3.2]
　　and he had put himself into the burlwood,
he drifted ashore in front of the town, they say,

to wait for Rockfacet's children to come to the beach.[6]

After a time, they came down to the tideline.
«Look! Driftwood has floated ashore!»
«Driftwood never floats ashore in father's village.
How fine that it's happened!»

They carried it up
and set it on the ground outside the doorway.   160
Then they forgot it.

As they were just getting ready for bed,
they remembered it,
and then they brought it in.

Their father started splitting it
with one of five stone axes that he owned.
The axehead broke, they say.

Then he took another.
He started to split it with that,
but it broke too.   170

After this happened to four of his axeheads,
he split it successfully with the last.
That made him happy, they say,
and he fed the wood to the fire.

Back of the screens, Rockfacet's daughters got into their beds,
and this one came out of the wood, they say.
He sat near the head [of the younger]
and reached out to touch her.
«Who is it?»

«It's me,» he replied.   180

«Who is *me*?»

«I am Spirit Being Living in the Little Finger.»

When he was whittling as a child,
something got stuck in his littlest finger, they say.
That's what gave him the name.

The woman said,
«My father sired me for him alone.»

Then she said it again,
and then he made love to her.

WHEN morning came,   190
        her father said,   [3.3]
«What spirit being could it be who was talking
        to my daughter in the night?
I sired her for no one but the Spirit Being
        Living in the Little Finger.»

«Father,» she answered,
«that is who he says he is.»

«Well, my darling, come here with your husband.»

Then they came to the fire and sat there, they say.
Her father spread out a mat for him
and started to offer him food.

They brought dried berries in a box.   200
Fire was seething inside them.
They put some into a tray
and set it before him.
The woman told him not to eat them.

After chewing on four medicine leaves,
he took some of the berries.
After filling his mouth twice,
he took no more.

They went through him, still burning.
When he stood up,   210
smoke was still rising from where he'd been sitting.

O N THE FOLLOWING DAY, they say,   [3.4]
    the father said to his daughter,
«Let your husband go inland
   to take down an alder I own and bring in the wood.»

He got out of bed at once.
She drew her husband aside.
«Ahhh! Where those who are spirit beings from birth think
       someone is strong,
they arrange for their children to marry.
But what if, a little bit later, they start to do this!»

Then he said to his wife,   220
«Let me go.
I would like to see just what he plans for me.»

Then she said to her husband,
«Wait till it flashes and crashes together four times
  before you go toward it.»

Then his wife's father gave him a stone wedge
and he started up a trail
leading inland from next to the house.
After walking a ways,
he saw it there before him in the distance.   230

After he had watched it for a while,
and it had flashed and crashed together four times,
he spat the medicine ahead of him
and went to it.

After he had chopped at it awhile,
as soon as it had fallen,
he found himself in its mouth.
He saw no way of escaping.
Something held him fast between its teeth.

Then he thought about his father's spirit powers.   240
Four of them came to him
with twigs of redcedar tied in their hair.
Two of them had wedges in their hands.
Two of them were carrying big mallets.

They spread the alder open,
and they held it with a strut.
Then they pulled him out.
He rubbed himself with medicine,
and then he was the way he'd been before.

When he pulled apart the jaws,   250
many people's skeletons fell out.
Flesh still clung to some of them.
Some were only ligaments and bones.

Then he stomped the alder into pieces
and scattered them around.
«This will be of use to the last people in the world.»

Then he carried a part of it off on his shoulder
and pulled out its teeth right in front of the house
and split it into pieces near the door.
Then, they say, his father-in-law said,   260

«Aiii! He has killed my spirit power.»

Then he went inside
and slept with his wife behind the screen.
His wife's father cursed the fire, they say.

O N THE FOLLOWING DAY, his wife's father   [3.5]
          spoke to her again.
«My dear, let your husband go and get
a little octopus I own, out on the point.»

He got straight out of bed once again,
and his wife drew him aside again and said,
«Where those who are spirit beings from birth think
          someone is strong,   270
they arrange for their children to marry.
But what if, a little bit later, they start to do this!»

Then he said to his wife,
«Let me go.
I will see once again what exactly he plans for me.»

Then she told her husband,
«Wait until it spouts and lightning flashes four times
before you go toward it.»

Then he went to it, they say.
He shot it twice, they say,   280
with the arrows he was given by his father.
⟨ He also took along a gaffhook   281a
that his wife's father offered him, they say.⟩[7]   281b

When it had spouted four times,
and he had spat the medicine ahead of him,
he went to it, they say.
After he had snagged it with the gaffhook,

he found himself in its mouth.

When he was close to drowning in its slime,
he thought of his father's spirit powers, they say.
Four of them came to him again.
They came with clubs   290
and pounded its eyes and its arms.

They pulled him out.
He was covered with slime.
He licked himself with medicine
and made himself the way he'd been before.
There were many people's skeletons in that one too, they say.

He tore the octopus in half
and ripped a part of it to shreds.
Then he scattered them around.
«These will be of use to the last people in the world.»   300

Then he dragged the rest of it back with the gaffhook, they say.
He dropped it near the door,
and his father-in-law said,
«Aiii! He has killed my spirit power.»

Then he went inside
and lay down beside his wife behind the screens, they say.

O N THE FOLLOWING DAY, his wife's father   [3.6]
      spoke to his daughter again.
«My dear, let your husband go and get
a small sea lion that I own, a little ways to seaward.»

He got right up.   310
Again she hugged her husband
and wept at the same time.

«Where those who are spirit beings from birth think
        someone is strong,
    they arrange for their children to marry.
    But what if, a little bit later, they start to do this!»

Then he said to his wife,
«Let me go.
    I will see once again what exactly he plans for me.»

Then she told her husband,
«Wait until it glares at you and growls four times   320
    before you go toward it.»

Then he went to get it.
He planned to kill it with a club
    that his father-in-law had offered him.

When he had gone a little ways,
he saw it
    roosting there.

After it had glared at him and growled four times,
he went nearer.
When he came up close to it,   330
it yawned,
    and then he found himself in its mouth.

He thought again about his father's spirit powers,
and they came to him again,
    dressed as hunters with bone clubs.
They hit the sea lion squarely on the head.
They clubbed it to death.

He appeared to be dead
    when they pulled him out of the sea lion's mouth.

He put the medicine into his mind   340
and it made him more careful.

Then he cut open the sea lion carcass.
⟨Four⟩ people's bones tumbled out.
He tore half of the carcass to pieces
and threw them around.
«Not even the last people in the world
        will fail to find you useful.»

And he carried half of the sea lion back
and threw it through the doorway.
«Aiii! He has killed my spirit power,»
his father-in-law said.   350
And again he lay down with his wife in back of the screens.

O N THE FOLLOWING DAY, his father-in-law   [3.7]
        spoke to his daughter again.
«My dear, let your husband go and get
a small harbour seal that I keep not far from here.»

He got up once again,
and again she hugged her husband and wept.
«Where those who are spirit beings from birth think
        someone is strong,
they arrange for their children to marry.
But what if, a little bit later, they start to do this!»

Then he said to his wife,   360
«Let me go.
I will see what exactly he plans for me.»

«Wait until it glares at you and growls four times
before you go toward it,»
she told him.

His father-in-law gave him another bone club,
and then he went after it.

When he came to the place,
and the seal had glared at him, growling four times,
he went up to it.   370
Then it inhaled him,
and he found himself in its mouth.

He thought of his father's spirit powers again.
Four of them came to help him again.
They carried bone clubs too.

They hit the seal on the head
and killed it.
Then they pulled him out
and he rubbed the medicine into his mind.

And then he ripped the seal in two.   380
He tore one half of it to pieces
and scattered it around.
«Even the last people in the world will find this useful too.»
⟨Three⟩ people's bones tumbled out of it, they say.

And he carried half the seal back on his shoulder
and plunked it in the house.
«Aiii! He has killed my spirit power,»
his father-in-law said.
And again, they say, he took his wife to bed
        in the place behind the screens.

O N THE FOLLOWING DAY, his wife's father said to her,   390
    «My dear, let your husband go and get   [3.8]
a little eagle that I keep not far from here.»

Again she asked her husband not to go,
and he said to his wife,
«I am going to go, the same as before.
I am going to see what exactly he plans for me.»

And she said to her husband,
«After the fourth blink of its innermost eyelid,
you can get close to it.»

They say he took along his father's arrows.   400
[«A digging stick,»] his father-in-law said.
«is the weapon they usually use.»

Then he went after it.
After the fourth blink of its innermost eyelid,
he shot it in the belly.
Then he went around the other side
and shot the second arrow from there.

He didn't use the digging stick, they say.
He killed it with the arrows.
Then he scattered half of it around.   410
«Even the last people in the world will find you useful.»

He carried the rest of it home on his shoulder.
In its belly there were two people's bones, they say.
He plunked it down in the house.

«Aiii! He has killed my spirit power,»
his father-in-law said.
And again he lay down with his wife.

ON THE FOLLOWING DAY, the father said   [3.9]
the same thing to his daughter once again.
«My dear, let your husband go and get a little clam
that I keep out on the point.»   420

She went to her husband just as before.
Nevertheless, he prepared to head out.
Then she told her husband what to do.
«Wait until it spits four times
before you go up close to it.»

«The weapon they normally use,»
said his father-in-law, «is a stick.»
And he gave him a digging stick.

Then he went to get it.
After it had spit four times,   430
and he had come up close to it
and had started using the digging stick,
he found himself in its jaws.

When he thought about his father's spirit powers,
they came to him.
Now they were carrying fishclubs.
They smashed the hinge of the clam,
and they lifted him out.

He scattered half of it around.
«Even the last people in the world will find this
            useful too,» he said.   440
⟨One person's bones were there inside of it, they say.⟩[8]   440a

He grabbed the rest of it
and dragged it home
and dropped it in the house.
«Aiii! He has killed my spirit power.»
And again he lay down with his wife.

O N THE FOLLOWING DAY, his father-in-law   [3.10]
        gave orders for building a fire.

They kindled the flame
by rubbing two nuggets of agate together.

Then he instructed them to put cooking rocks into the fire.
They did as he said.   450
When the stones were hot,
they transferred them with tongs to a big stone basin
        ⟨full of water⟩ near the door.
Then the old man told him to get in, they say.

He stood up at once.
After spitting the medicine into it four times,
he did get in.
The water was cool.

Then they put a cover on the basin.
After he had sat in there awhile,
he tapped against the sidewall.   460

His wife's father snorted and twiddled his lips at him.
«I guess I have killed him with this,»
his father-in-law said.

Later he stood, breaking the lid with his head.
Then he stamped the lid to pieces in the basin
and dragged the basin out the door, they say.

The old man was embarrassed.
The young man had annihilated ten spirit powers.[9]
So the old man changed his mind
        about his son-in-law, they say.

The octopus he killed was in the cave
        at Qquuna Point, they say.   470
And his wife's father, Rockfacet Cliff, rises
        behind the village of Qquuna.[10]   471

,　　　,　　　,

AFTER he had lived there as a married man awhile,　　　473
　　he mentioned to his wife　　　　　　　　　　　　　　[4.1]
that he would like to see his home again.

She told this to her father,
and her father said,
«My dear, you should go with your husband.
The canoe is right outside.»

Then her husband went outside.　　　　　　　　　480
The carcass of an old canoe was lying there
with grass growing up through the cracks in the hull.

Then he came in
and he spoke to his wife,
and she spoke to her father in turn.
«Father, he was unable to find the canoe.
There is only an old overgrown one, he says.»

«That's it.»

She went to it with her husband.
She stamped her foot beside it.　　　　　　　　490
«Go seaward, father's canoe.»

Then it floated offshore.
It went upwind and down on its own.
The carving on the bow knew what to do.
Then she called it to come near.
It came and floated right in front of her.

The old man told his daughter to pack boxes full of every
　　　　　kind of food.
There was a great supply.

He sent five slaves with the canoe.
He also had them pack five crates of oiled fruit[11]
    for the canoe.   500

Then he said to his daughter,
«My dear, whenever it gets hungry,
    the bow will come about and face astern.
Your husband has to pour a crate of fruit
    out right before its eyes.»

THEN they headed off, they say.   [4.2]
    He sat amidships with his wife,
and the carving on the bow knew what to do.

When they had travelled for a ways,
the bow of the canoe came about and faced astern.
They pulled out one container of the fruit,   510
and he fed it to the prow of the canoe.
Then they continued on their way.

When they had travelled on a ways,
the bow came about.
Again he fed oiled fruit to the prow of the canoe,
and the canoe went on its way.

When they had travelled on a ways,
they could almost see the town.
The smoke from the housefires rose like the teeth of a comb.

The villagers were keen to see Rockfacet's daughter.   520
«Who is it?» they asked.
«It's Spirit Being Living in the Little Finger
    coming with his wife.»

The people came down to the beach in a crowd,
[and when he and his wife stepped ashore,][12]   524a

they unloaded the cargo.
Then the canoe and its five slaves headed back.
They took the three remaining crates of fruit
to feed to the canoe.

H IS WIFE sat on top of the pile of cargo. [4.3]
    He walked to the house 530
to ask his mother to come and invite her inside.

His mother went down right away,
but there was no one to be seen.
There was only a cloud perched on the top of the boxes.

She went back inside,
and she said to her son,
«I saw nothing there.
There is only a cloud perched on the boxes.»

«That would be her,» he said to his mother.

She went down again 540
and invited her up.
His mother came in with the cloud close behind her.
Then the cloud kept on moving
and stopped at the place where her husband was sitting.

They were eager to see her.
A crowd had gathered to greet her.
After a time, he said to his wife,
«You could take off your hat.»

Then she asked her husband to take it off.
He lifted it up 550
and put it behind him.

The cloud disappeared,
and something amazing sat in its place,
lovely like a spirit being's daughter.

Those who had hoped they would marry him
stared at her, they say,
and after seeing her, they wept.

       ➤   ➤   ➤

AFTER he had lived there, married, for a while,   [5.1]
   a silver otter[13] swam in front of town, they say.
After some of them had shot at it awhile,   560
he launched his own canoe, they say.
He shot an arrow at it too.

He hit it right in the tip of the tail.
It thrashed around a long time in the water
before he was able to bring it aboard.
Then he came to shore with it.
He skinned it.

There were bloodstains on the pelt,
so his wife set out to wash it.
After she had worked at it awhile,   570
it started slipping out to sea,
and she went with it.

As the water reached her knees,
a killer whale took her seaward, spouting.
She was caught between its dorsal fins.[14]
The killer whale carried her away.

He launched his canoe
and went after his wife.
She vanished right in front of him.

Then he turned back   580
and wandered through the village, weeping.

Later on, he talked to an old man   [5.2]
  who lived at the edge of the village.
«What spirit being was it
  who took my wife away?» he asked.

«Spirit Being Staying in the Cradle is the one
  who took your wife,» he said.

Then the old man gave him useful things.
He gave him all the things
  it would be good for him to have.

«Now, sir, borrow my canoe.   590
  I'll go with you too,
  and I'll stay with the boat at the head of the trail
  while you go looking for your wife,»
  the old man said.

Then he lent him the stubby canoe
  that was sitting outside.

«Set it up on skids, sir.
  Scour and polish the hull.
  And get cedar-limb line and Haida tobacco and tallow.»

He did these things without delay.   600

Now the moment the weather was fair,   [5.3]
  he went to get the older man,
but the older one said that the weather was foul.

When the fog was thick,
he went to him anyway.

The old one was waiting outside with his paddler's mat
        on his shoulder.
He wore his sunhat too.

«It is excellent weather, my lord.
    On the open sea will be nothing but sunshine.»

He launched the canoe.   610
The older man got in the stern.
At once they set off.

When they had paddled out a ways,
just as he said,
there was sunshine.

The older one said to the younger,
«Sir, keep watch for a two-headed kelp.»

Then they paddled up beside one.
«Leave me here, with this for a moorage.
This is the trail that leads where she is.»   620

And then the old man told him what to do.
«At the edge of the village, right on the trail, a heron
        keeps repairing a canoe.
He never lets a foreign spirit being pass.

«When he shouts, you have to act quickly.
Put Haida tobacco into his mouth,
and give him the cedar-limb line.
Then he will hide you.»

After that, he went down on the kelp stipe.

AFTER following the footsteps on the trail for a time,   [5.4.1]
   he heard the sound of steady tapping.   · 630
Then he came upon the heron.
The heron watched him for a moment.
Then the heron shouted.

He put tobacco in the heron's mouth
and handed him cedar-limb line.
Then the heron closed his beak,
and he was hidden there inside, they say.

A crowd came running toward the heron from the village.
«Why did you call out?»

«My chisel slipped.   640
   That's why I called out.»

«No!» they said.
«You stink of human being.»

They searched him
but found no one.
Then they returned to the town, all in a bunch.

The heron opened up his beak and brought him out
and told him what to do.

«Spirit Being Staying in the Cradle took your wife.
   His three-headed housepole[15] is always on watch.   650
   Don't let it see you.
   Did you think to bring some tallow?»

«Yes,» he said.

«Two people covered head to toe with scabs will soon come
       out for firewood.

Heal their skin.
Rub them with tallow.»
Then this one went back of the village, they say.

W HEN he'd been sitting there awhile,   [5.4.2]
    the two of them came toward him.

They called to him.   660
«Don't tickle us with your eyes!» they said.
They told him he should show himself.
Then he went right up to them, they say.
He rubbed them with the tallow.

Then the two of them said to him,
«Tonight they are putting a dorsal fin on your wife.
That's why we've been sent to gather firewood.

«This evening, when we're sent to get fresh water,
    we'll arrange it so our bucket handles break.
We'll spill the water so that it runs into the fire.   670
Search for your wife in the midst of the steam.»
That's what they said to him.

A S SOON AS evening came,   [5.4.3]
    they came out with two big buckets to get water.
He watched them.
«Get ready,»
they said to him.

When they brought in the water,
he looked at his wife through the doorway.
There were tearstains on her cheeks.   680
They had laced up her bridegroom,
        Spirit Being Staying in the Cradle,
so his arms lay close against his sides.[16]

W HEN the two of them came close beside the fire,   [5.4.4]
      one on either side,
their bucket handles broke.

While the house was full of steam,
he raced inside and got his wife.
Then he put her in his armpit
and ran out.

The heads of the housepole yelled,
«Spirit Being Living in the Little Finger
      is running away with his wife!»   690

T HEY WENT after him at once.   [5.4.5]
      A horde of them went after him.
Spirit Being Staying in the Cradle wanted
      to fight him, they say.

He reached the heron, carrying his wife.
Again, the heron hid him in his beak.
And then the rest of them arrived.

They hollered,
«Hey, old man! Didn't Spirit Being Living in the Little Finger
      pass this way?
He's taken back his wife!»

«Haven't seen a thing,» the heron said.   700

They searched around,
and after they had searched,
they questioned him again,
«Didn't you see anything?»

«Nothing,» he replied.

Then they said to him,
«You stink of human being.»

They knocked him down.
They frisked him.
Then he said to them,   710
«You're boring me.
  Quit pushing me around.»

Then they left him and went back.

Then the heron put him down again, together with his wife.
  And then the heron said,
«Take this trail with your wife – and watch your step.»

T HEY STARTED OUT together on the trail then,   [5.5]
        they say.
After they had gone along together for a time,
they reached the place
where he had left the old man waiting in the boat, they say. 720

They climbed aboard with him and paddled.
After they had paddled for a ways,
he stepped ashore, they say, at his own village, with his wife.
He was glad to have his wife back,
and he stayed with her from that day on, they say.

This is where it ends.[17]   726

In His Father's Village,
Someone
Was Just About to Go Out
Hunting Birds[1]

T
HERE WAS A CHILD OF GOOD FAMILY, they say.   [1]
He wore two marten-skin blankets.
After he took up the shooting of birds,
he went inland, uphill from the village, they say.

Going through the pines,
just to where the ponds lay,
he heard geese calling.
Then he went in that direction.

There were two women bathing in a lake.
Something lay there on the shore.   10
Two goose skins were thrown over it.
Under their tails were patches of white.

After watching for a while,
he swooped in.
He sat on the two skins.
The women asked to have them back.

He asked the better-looking one to marry him.
The other one replied.
«Don't marry my younger sister.
I am smarter. Marry me.»   20

«No. I will marry your younger sister.»

And she said that she accepted him, they say.

«Well then! Marry my younger sister.
  You caught us bathing in a lake
  that belongs to our father.
  Now give me my skin.»

He gave it back.
She slipped it on
while she was swimming in the lake.

A goose swam in the lake then,   30
and then she started calling.
And then she flew, they say,
though leaving her younger sister
sickened her heart.

She circled above them.
Then she flew off, they say.
She passed through the sky.

He gave the younger woman one of his marten-skin blankets,
and he brought her home, they say.

A two-headed redcedar stood at the edge of the village,   40
and he put his wife's skin between the trunks.
Then he brought her into his father's house.

THE HEADMAN'S SON had taken a wife.   [2.1]
  So his father invited the people, they say.
They offered her food.
She did nothing but smell it.
She would eat no human food.

Later, her husband's mother started steaming silverweed,[2]
    they say.
Then she paid closer attention.
When her husband's mother was still busy cooking,   50
she asked her husband
to ask her to hurry, they say.

They placed it before her.
It vanished.
And then they began to feed her this only, they say.

AFTER A TIME, as he was sleeping,   [2.2]
his wife lay down beside him, and her skin was cold.
When it happened again,
he decided to watch her, they say.

He lay still in the bed,   60
and he felt her moving away from him slowly, they say.
Then she went out.
He followed behind her.

She walked along the beach in front of the village.
She went where the skin was kept.
From there, she flew.
She landed beyond the point at the edge of town.

He started toward her.
She was eating the eelgrass[3] that grew there,
and the breaking waves were lifting her back toward shore.   70
He saw her, they say.
And then she flew back where they kept her skin.

He got back to the house
before she did, they say.
There he lay down,
and soon his wife lay down beside him, cold.

A FAMINE began in the village, they say.   [2.3]
    One day, without leaving her seat, she said,
«My father is sending things down through the clouds to me.»

Back of the village, geese began landing and honking.   80
She went there.
They followed her.
Food of many kinds was lying there:
silverweed and clover roots.[4]
They carried it home.
And her father-in-law invited the people, they say.

When that was entirely gone,
    she said it again:
«My father is sending things down through the clouds to me.»
    Geese began landing and honking again
            in back of the village.   90

They went there.
There were piles, again, of many kinds of food.
Again they brought it home.
And her father-in-law again invited the people.

Then, they say, someone in the village said,
«She thinks very highly of goose food.»

The woman heard it.
She got up to leave at that moment, they say.
Her husband tried to dissuade her.
No use.   100
She had settled on leaving.

It was the same when he tried to dissuade her
            in front of the town.
She went where her skin was.
Then she flew.

74

She flew in circles over the town,
and leaving her husband sickened her heart, they say.

And then she passed through the sky.
After that, her husband was constantly weeping, they say.

AN OLD MAN had a house at the edge of the village.   [3]
He went there and asked,   110
«Don't you know the trail that leads to my wife?»

«Headman's son, you married a woman whose mother
        and father are not of this world.»

And the old man began to fit him out.
He gave him a bone marlinspike for working
        with cedar-limb line.
Then he said,
«Now, sir, get some oil.
Get two sharp wedges too.
And a comb and a cord and salmon roe and a coho skin
        and a spearhead.
Get all these.»

After he had gathered what he needed,   120
he came back to him, they say.
«Old one, here are all the things you spoke of.»

«Now, sir, you may go.
Take the narrowest of the trails that lead from my house.»
Then he set off.

AFTER walking awhile,   [4.1]
he came upon someone infested with lice.
He was trying to catch the lice by turning around.

After he had stared at him awhile,
the other said,   130
«Sir, don't just tickle me with your eyes.
I've been waiting a long time for you.»

Then he went up close,
and he combed out his hair.
He rubbed him with oil
and picked off the lice.
And he gave him the comb and the rest of the oil.

The other one said,
«This is the trail that leads to your wife.»

AGAIN he set off.   140
    After walking awhile,   [4.2.1]
he saw a small mouse in front of him.
There was a cranberry in her mouth.

Then she came to a fallen tree,
and she looked for a way to go over it.
He let her step onto his open hand
and put her across.

She laid her tail up between her ears
and ran ahead.
Not far away, she went under some ferns.   150

He rested there,   [4.2.2]
and something said,
«A headwoman asks if you wish to come in.»
Then he parted the fronds of the ferns.

He was standing in front of a large house.
He walked through the door.
There was the headwoman dishing up cranberries.

She spoke with grace.
Her voice had big round eyes.

After she'd offered him something to eat,   160
Mouse Woman said to him,   [4.2.3]
«When I was bringing a bit of a cranberry back
          from my berry patch,
, you helped me.
 I intend to lend you something that I wore
for stalking prey when I was younger.»

She brought out a box.
She pulled out four more boxes within boxes.
In the innermost box was the skin of a mouse
          with small bent claws.
She said to him,
«Put this on.»   170

Small though it was, he got into it.
It was easy.
He went up the wall and into the roof of the house.
And Mouse Woman said to him,
«You know what to do when you wear it.
Be on your way.»

H E S E T O U T again on the trail.   [4.3]
      After walking awhile,
he heard someone grunting and straining.
He went there.   180

A woman was hoisting a pile of stones.
The cedar-limb line she was using kept slipping.
He watched her awhile
and then he went up to her.

«Excuse me,» he said,
«but what are you doing?»

The woman replied,
«They told me to hold up the mountains of the Islands
            on the Boundary between Worlds.
That is what I am doing.»

Then he remembered his spruce-root cord   190
and he said, «Let me help you.»

He made splices with the cord.
«Now take the load on your back,» he said,
 and she hoisted it up on her back.
It did not slip off.

 And she said to him,
«Sir, you have helped me.
Here is the trail that leads to your wife.»

Then he went on.

A FTER A TIME, he came to a hump in the muskeg.   200
      Something slender and red grew from the top of it. [4.4.1]
He went up close to it.
All around the bottom of the tall, thin thing lay human bones.

He saw no way of going up.
Then he entered the mouse skin.
Pushing the salmon roe ahead of him, he climbed.
He went up after it.
When he came to the top,
he pulled himself onto the sky.

The trail stretched ahead of him there too.   210
He walked along.   [4.4.2]

After travelling awhile,
he started to hear a bubbling sound.

After travelling further,
he came to a river.
It was running high.

Near it perched an eagle.
A heron perched on the opposite bank.
A kingfisher perched upstream.
A black bear sat on the opposite bank,   220
and he had no claws, they say.

Then, they say, the black bear said to the eagle,
«Lend me something, grandfather.»
Then, they say, the eagle did as he asked.
Then and there the black bear got his claws.

When the young man had been sitting there awhile,   [4.4.3]
half of a person lurched by,
leaning himself on a fishing spear.

He had one leg and one arm,
and his head was half a head.   230
He speared the coho that were swimming there
and put them into his basket.[5]

The man unrolled his coho skin and put it on
and swam in that direction.
When the half man speared him,
he was unable to pull him in.

The young man cut the spearhead from the spear, they say.
And the half man said,
«Human beings sometimes do this sort of thing.»

The younger man went up to him then, they say.   240
«Sir, did something take your spearhead?»

«Yes,» he said.

And the young man gave him the one he had.
That was Stickwalking God, they say.

WHEN he went up further,   [4.5]
two men, old and fat, came out collecting firewood.
They chopped at the roots of windfall trees,
and they scattered the chips on the water.
The coho were coming from there.

He went back of the fallen tree,   250
pushing stones in from behind,
and their wedges shattered, they say.
And one of them said,
«Ooooow! We'll get a beating!»

Then he went up to them.
He gave them the two wedges that he had.
And they stared at him and said,
«This is your wife's house.»

He went up to it, they say.
He stood waiting in front of the house.   260
His wife came out to meet him.

He went in with her.
She was happy to see him.
She was the village headman's daughter, they say.

In that village too, they were man and wife.
And everything they gathered,
he gathered as well.

AFTER living there for a time, [5.1]
he began to dislike the entire country.
Then his wife spoke to her father. 270
And his father-in-law called the villagers in.
There in the house, he asked them, they say,
«Who will carry my son-in-law back?»

And a loon said,
«I will carry your son-in-law back.»

«How will you do it?» he asked.

The loon said,
«I will put him under my tail
and dive right in front here.
Then I'll come up again at the edge of his father's town 280
and release him.»

They thought he was too weak to do it, they say.

His father-in-law asked the question again. [5.2]
A grebe gave the same reply.
They thought she was also too weak.

And a raven said he would carry him back. [5.3]
And they asked him, «How will you do it?»

«I will put him under my wing
and fly with him from the edge of the village.
When I'm tired, 290
I'll let myself tumble and fall with him.»

They were pleased with his answer, they say,
and they all came down to the edge of the village to watch.

He did as he said.   [5.4]
When he grew tired,
he let himself fall down through the clouds with him
and dropped him onto a shoal exposed by the tide.

«Hwuuu! What a load I have carried.»

Becoming a gull, he squawked and went on squawking.   [5.5]

This is where it ends.   300

The Sea Lion Hunter[1]

A MASTER CARVER HAD FATHERED [1]
two children, they say.

They saw game on the reefs,
so he made the harpoon.
He bound it with cord, they tell me.
He used something strong for this purpose, they say.
And he put a detachable barb on the shaft.

They herded the sea lions into a pool on top of a reef,
and he was the one who harpooned them.
One thrust, and he pulled out the shaft
and fastened another barb on the end.   10
This is the way he killed sea lions, they say.

When he had been doing this for a while,
they paddled out early one day
and they put him ashore on the reef.
Then they pushed off
and left him.

His wife's youngest brother turned toward him.
There in the midst of the crew, he tugged at their paddles.
He struggled against them.

The hunter was watching.   20
He called them again and again.
They paid no attention.

They were unable to kill the sea lions.
He was the only one who could do it.
That is the reason they left him, they say.

Alone on the top of the rock, he wept for his children.
He wept for a while,
and then he lay down by the pool.

After he lay there in silence awhile,
something said to him,   30
«A headman asks you in.»

He looked around him.
Nothing stood out,
but he noticed that, there in the pool, something went under.

When he had lain there a little while longer,
something said the same thing again.
Then, they say, he peeked through the eye
of the marten-skin cape he was wearing.
Then he saw a pied bill grebe break the surface of the pool.

After swimming there awhile,   40
it said, «A headman asks you in,»
and then it went under.

H E WRAPPED his fingers round the whetstone   [2]
that he wore around his neck,
and he leaped into the pool, they say.

He found himself in front of a large house,
and they invited him inside.

He went in,
and there they asked him,
«Why is it you are murdering so many of my women?»[2]   50

He answered,
«I have done what I have done
in order to give food to my two children.»

In a pool in a corner of the house,
he saw two baby killer whales spouting.
Those, they say, were the headman's children, playing.
In all four corners of the house, he saw the dorsal fins
          of killer whales
hanging up in bunches.

Then, however, they offered him food.
There was a sea lion sitting near the door.   60
They dragged it to the center.

They lifted the cooking rocks out of the fire
and dropped them down its throat.
They dropped a halibut down the throat of the sea lion too.
When the halibut was cooked, they say,
they set it there before him.

When the meal was over,
they brought one of the fins down from the corner.
They heated the base of the fin.

When they made him bend over,   70
he slung the whetstone around so it hung down his back.
When they tried to fasten the fin to his spine,
it fell off.
The fin lay on the stone floorplanks, quivering.

They went to get another.
They heated that one also, right away,
and they forced him to bend over.

Again he moved the whetstone.
When they tried to fasten the fin to his spine,
it fell off like the other,   80
and it dropped onto the stone floor of the house.

Then they got another.
When the same thing happened yet again,
they went and got a tall one.[3]

After they had warmed it there awhile,
they forced him to bend over once again.
He moved the whetstone round again.
When they tried to fasten that one to his spine,
it too fell shuddering on the stone floor of the house.

After they had tried four times,   90
    they gave it up.
«Let him go,» the headman said.
«He refuses the fin.
    Put him into a sea lion's belly.»

Then the headman told him what to do.
«After you have drifted here and there awhile,
    and after you have washed ashore four times,
    let yourself out.
You will find that you have come to a fine country.»

They put him into a sea lion's paunch right away.   100
He sewed it shut from the inside,
    and they set him adrift.

W HEN he had floated on the ocean for a while   [3]
      and washed ashore for the fourth time,
he crawled out.
He had drifted ashore on a sandy beach.

He sewed the paunch up tight from the outside,
and he put it in the water.
It faced upwind
and disappeared to seaward.   110

Then he walked in the direction of the village.
He waited until nightfall on the outskirts of the town.
After dark, he peeked in at his wife.

His wife had singed her hair off.
He saw soot stains on her face.[4]
He saw that both his children sat there too.

He tapped against the wall just opposite his wife.
She came outside.
He said to her, «Bring me my tools.»

She brought him what he asked for.   120
«Don't tell anyone I'm here,» he said.
«Don't even tell the children.»

When he left that place,
he grabbed another of the children who were playing there.
He took the child up the hill.

A FTER walking for a while,   [4.1]
     he came to a big lake.
There was a tall redcedar standing on the shore.

He cut the trunk across the front.

When he made another cut across the back,   130
the cedar dropped across the surface of the water.

He split it from the butt end.
After splitting it part way,
he braced it open.

Then he stripped and twisted cedar limbs,
splicing them together to make line.
When the line was long enough,
he tied the child to one end.
Then he lowered it into the lake between
        the split halves of the tree.

After letting it touch bottom,   140
he jigged with it awhile.
Then the line began to jerk,
and he began to haul it in.
By then the lake was boiling.

Its forepaws broke the surface first.
When its head broke the surface just behind them,
he sprang the trap by kicking out the brace.

The creature thrashed and struggled.
He clubbed it again and again,
until he had killed it.   150

Then he pulled it from the trap.
He touched his knifepoint to its throat,
but then a lightning bolt exploded,
so he started his cut instead from the base of the tail.

He skinned it.
He liked the way its tail looked especially.
It was curled.

Then he built a fire,
and he dried and tanned the skin.
It was a Seawolf that he caught, they say.   160

After he had tanned it,
he rolled it up
and packed it back to town.

On the outskirts of town stood a hollow redcedar.
He hid it in there.
He put moss over top of it.

T HEN he walked away from the edge of the village.   [4.2]
  He carved redcedar into the forms of killer whales.
He fitted them with dorsal fins
and pushed them under water with his feet
        and let them go.   170

Just out beyond low tide mark, some bubbles rose.
Then he said, «You're on your own.
Go wherever you can live.»

Those are harbour porpoises, they say.[5]

Next he carved some western hemlock
into the forms of killer whales.
When he had ten of them,
he pushed them under water with his feet and let them go.

After they had left,
bubbles rose a little farther seaward.
After that he turned it over in his mind.   180

Then he said, «You're on your own.
Go wherever you can live.»
Those are Dall's porpoises, they say.[6]

All this time, the weather was good, they say,
and as long as it lasted, the men were out fishing.

O N THE FOLLOWING DAY, after thinking again   [4.3]
   about what he would use,
he made ten killer whales out of yew wood.

Their skins were shiny black and splashed with white,
their underbellies white,   190
and they had white patches up behind their mouths.

The dorsal fin of one was nicked along the fore edge.
The dorsal fin of one hooked backward toward the tail.
As he was making them, they moved.

He laid down skids for them to rest on.
Then he launched them,
and he pushed them with his feet to deeper water.
Bubbles rose a long time later, out at sea.

Then he called them in
and hauled them up on shore.   200
They had snapper, salmon and halibut in their jaws.

E VENING came again,   [4.4]
   and he went to see his wife.
Once again he peeked inside,
and then he tapped on the wall beside his wife.
She came outside.

He said to her, «Tell your youngest brother
he ought to wear a feather in his hair
when the men go fishing in the morning.»

Next day, when they were fishing,   210
he gave the killer whales their instructions.

«Do away with all the humans who are fishing.
  Rub your fins on their canoes,
  and only save the one who wears a feather in his hair.»

Then he nudged them to sea with his feet, they say.
  Bubbles rose a while later,
  seaward of where the canoes were riding at anchor.

Then the killer whales closed in on the canoes.
  Bubbles rose among the boats.
  The killer whales rubbed against them with their fins   220
  and chewed the canoes and humans to pieces.
  Only one, who wore a feather in his hair,
          continued swimming.

When the whales had destroyed them all,
  the one who wore a feather in his hair climbed aboard
          a chewed canoe,
  and the pod of whales brought him to the shore.
  They left him on the beach in front of town.

THEN he called the killer whales again.   [4.5]
  He told them what to do.

He said to one who had a knothole in his fin,
  «Pierced Fin will be your name.»   230
    To one whose fin was wavy, he said,
  «Your name will be Rippled Fin.»[7]

Then he told them this:
  «Go to House Point.
    Make your homes there.
    That is a fine country.
    People of the Strait will be your name.»

Then he went to see his wife
with fish the killer whales had brought him in their mouths.
Both of his children were happy to see him.   240

WHEN he had been in the village awhile,   [5.1]
     he went outside
while others were still sleeping.

He dressed in the Seawolf skin.
There at the edge of the village, he reached out and touched
     the water with one paw,
and he had half of a spring salmon.

His mother-in-law, who nagged him all the time,
always got up early in the morning.
He laid the salmon down at the door of her house.

Early in the morning, she came out.   250
She found the chunk of salmon
and was happy.

That night again, he dressed in the Seawolf skin.
He went into the water up to the elbow.
He came back with half a halibut.

He set it down beside his mother-in-law's door.
She found it in the morning.
The people of the village had been hungry up till then,
     they say.

Again that night, he dressed in the skin of the Seawolf.
He put his foreleg all the way into the water,   260
and he got a whole spring salmon.
He set it at the woman's door as well,
and she found it in the morning.

He dressed again the next night in the Seawolf skin,
and then he let the water come over his back.
He brought in the jaw of a humpback whale
and left it at his mother-in-law's door.
She was very pleased to find it there.

H IS MOTHER-IN-LAW started to perform   [5.2]
    as a shaman then, they say.
They fasted side by side with her for four nights.   270
He was with them too, they say.
It was his voice that started speaking through her –
through the mother of his wife.

The next night again, he got inside the Seawolf.
He swam seaward.
He killed a humpback whale.
Fangs stuck out of the nostrils of the Seawolf.
Those are what he killed it with, they say.

He put it up between his ears
and carried it to shore.   280
He put it down in front of the house.
She had predicted
that a whale would appear.

And again, as they were sleeping,
he went out inside the Seawolf.
He got a pair of humpback whales.

He brought them back to shore.
He carried one between his ears
and the other draped across the base of his tail.
He swam ashore with them   290
and set them down again in front of the house.

When night came again,
he swam way out to sea inside the Seawolf.
He got ten humpback whales.

He carried several bundled up between his ears.
He carried others in a bunch at the base of his tail.
He had them piled on his body,
and he put one in his mouth.
He started swimming toward the shore.

He was still out at sea when daylight came, they say,   300
and when he came up on the beach,
the mother of his wife was there to meet him
        in the headdress of a shaman.

He stepped outside the Seawolf skin.
«Why,» he asked her, «are there spearpoints in your eyes?
Does the spirit being speaking through you
get some help from me?»
She died of shame from what he said, they say.

THE SEAWOLF SKIN swam out to sea alone.   [5.3]
    Then the hunter took the string of whales
and said that no one was to touch them.   310

The sale of those whales made him rich, they say.
And then he held ten feasts in honor, so they say,
        of the youngest brother of his wife.
He made a prince of him.

This is where it ends.[8]

The One Who Got Rid
of Nine of His Nephews[1]

ONE WHO WAS THE MOTHER OF A TOWN [1]
      kept starting to arrange
           to let his nephews take his wife, they say.[2]
Then he led them out and they were gone forever more.
He said he had some firewood he wanted brought inside,
and they were gone forever more.

He said he had some bark[3] and some cormorants as well,
and then he sent them out with nets,
and they were gone forever more.

He did it over and over again,
until nine of them had disappeared, they say.
And the youngest one began to understand. 10

The youngest started to bathe himself, they say.
When he had bathed himself awhile,
he grew strong.

Anything he squeezed
just shattered in his hands.
If he twisted the limb of a spruce,
he pulled it clean out of the tree.

When he became extremely strong,
he started making things, they say.

He made a pair of hard, sharp wedges   20
Then he got a giant mussel[4] shell.
He made it into a razor.
And then he got a weasel skin,
and then he got a feather.

Then he took a lump of wet clay
and shaped it with a pocket in the middle.
He shaped it so that he could go inside.

Then he bathed himself again
and he sat on the top of the house.

After he had sat there for a while,   30
his uncle came outside, they say.
When his uncle discovered him up there
his uncle hurried back inside.

His uncle felt uneasy then, they say.
He sent someone out to call his nephew in.
And then he came, they say.

He went inside,
and his uncle spread a mat for him.
After he had offered him some food, he said,
«Nephew, you are the one who should marry my wife.»   40
And that night, he slept with her, they say.

NEXT DAY his uncle said,   [2.1]
    «Nephew, I have firewood out back.
I want it brought into the house.»

The nephew hid the wedges in his clothes.
His uncle led the way.
He walked along behind.

His uncle pried open a dry tree
and then put something in to brace it.
Then his uncle dropped his own wedge down the crack,
      they say,   50
and told his nephew to go get it.

He went inside the tree to get the wedge, they say.
His uncle knocked the brace out,
and the crack snapped shut, they say.

His uncle was delighted.
«Look at that!
  That's the end of the one who intended to marry my wife.»
He heard his uncle say it.
Then his uncle walked away.

Then he pushed his wedges through, they say,   60
and split the tree from the inside.
Then he stepped out
and broke it into pieces.
His older brothers' bones were there inside.

He stomped on half of it and scattered it around.
He carried the rest of it home on his shoulder
and threw it down in the house.

That was his uncle's power, they say.
And then again he slept with his uncle's wife.

NEXT DAY his uncle said to him, they say,   70
   «Nephew, come with me.   [2.2]
We'll go and get some cormorants.
I own some that are perching over there.»

He took along the weasel skin and feather,
and went hunting with his uncle.

At the top of a tall cliff a log was sticking out.
From there his uncle dropped the net.
The cormorant was trapped in it.
And his uncle said to him,
«Now, nephew, your turn.»   80

When he stepped out on the log,
his uncle pushed him over.

He tucked himself inside the feather,
and then he floated down.
He heard his uncle singing,
«Look at that!
That's the end of the one who intended to marry my wife.»
And his uncle went away.

Then he dressed in his weasel skin
and climbed back up the cliff.   90
He dropped the net again, and again, and again.
He caught the whole flock of cormorants.

After catching all of them,
he tore the nets to shreds
and scattered all the pieces.

He dragged the cormorants back
and dragged them into the house.
Those were his uncle's powers, they say.
⟨And again he slept with his uncle's wife.⟩

THE NEXT DAY he went to get bark
     with his uncle, they say.   [2.3]
He hid what he had made.   100
He walked behind his uncle.
⟨His uncle built a fire there   101a
to steam the bark, they say.⟩⁵   101b

102

When the bark had cooked awhile,
his uncle picked some up.
He reached out to take some too,
and his uncle pushed him in.

Then he tucked himself inside the clay container he had made.
He didn't feel the burning,
but he heard his uncle singing,
«Look at that!
   That's the end of the one who intended to marry my wife.»   110

When his uncle went away,
he came back out.
He pushed away the bark
and scattered it around
and carried the rest of it home on his shoulder
and tossed it down in the house.
That too was his uncle's power, they say.
And again he slept with his uncle's wife.

T HE NEXT DAY again his uncle said,   [2.4]
   «Nephew, come with me.   120
I have some cockles.[6]
I want them brought up to the house.»
Then he went with him.
He took along his mussel-shell knife, they say.

The cockle opened its mouth.
His uncle told him to get it,
and when he went to get it,
his uncle pushed him in.
And again his uncle was pleased.
«Look at that!   130
   That's the end of the one who intended to marry my wife.»

When his uncle went away,
he cut the muscles of the cockle
so the shell fell open.

He scattered half of it around
and lifted the rest of it up on his shoulder
and threw it down in the house.
He had killed his uncle's powers, they say.

THEN his uncle spread out the skin of a black bear.   [2.5]
He invited him to sleep there, they say.   140

And when he did fall asleep there,
his uncle picked him up
and put him in a box.
He tied it with cords.

He took him far out to sea, they say.
And then he put him overboard.
And again his uncle was pleased,
and he paddled home.

AFTER drifting awhile,   [3.1]
he felt himself washing ashore.   150
When he was just getting ready to burst the box,
he heard two women speaking lovely words to one another.

One was saying,
«Cloudwatcher, a box has washed ashore.»
And he heard her,
and he did not burst the box.

The two women lifted up the lid,
and they helped him out.
Cloudwatcher's elder sister said,

«I'm the one who saw him first,   160
   and I'm the one who is going to marry him.»

Then they took him home.
They took him into their father's house,
and they treated him well.

After they had given him something to eat,
he went outside.
He walked through the town for a while,
and then he went into the middle house.

Eagle skins were hanging there.
He took down one with lovely feathers,   170
and then he put it on.

He moved his wings.
He almost sailed through the doorway.
He stopped himself by grabbing onto the frame.
He took the skin off right away.

Then he went back to the house of his father-in-law.
   His father-in-law was saying,
«It's funny. My skin tickles,
   just the way it does when there is someone else inside.»
He was the mother of the town, they say.   180

NEXT DAY early in the morning,   [3.2]
         he heard an eagle scream.
He went outside to look, they say.
There was something set up in front of the house.
Eagles were perched on it in a row.
They were calling each other
and sharpening their talons.
Then they went out hunting.

Later in the day, they came back in.
Some of them were carrying spring salmon.
Others were carrying red snapper. 190
Others had humpback whale.

A GAIN the next day, early, he heard them [3.3]
        calling in front of the house.
He told his wife he wanted to go hunting too.

She spoke to her father, they say.
And her father said,
«My dear, I will lend your husband
  something that I wore when I was young.»

He brought out a box.
He pulled out one with lovely feathers,
and he gave it to his daughter, 200
and he said to her,
«Tell your husband never to go near the little thing
      sticking out nearby.»

T HEN he went out with them, flying. [3.4]
  He brought in part of a humpback whale.
He flew home ahead of all the others,
and they brought in many kinds of things.
His father-in-law was pleased with him.
Then they cooked the whale.

When the food was served,
they led in an old woman, shaking with age. 210
They said to her,
«Drink whale broth, old woman.»
And she did that very thing.

H E FLEW with them again the following day. [3.5]
  He was starting to get used to it.

And he brought in the jaw of a humpback whale.
In his other claw, he carried a spring salmon.

He flew home ahead of them all.
They brought back many kinds of things.
And again when they served the whale,   220
they brought the old woman in,
and she drank the whale broth.

NEXT DAY, when he went out with them again,   [4]
he touched whatever it was that was sticking out.
And he grabbed hold of it, they say.
He flapped his wings awhile, holding steady.
Then it drew him down beneath the waves.

Another eagle seized his wings.
When that one too was about to go under,
one of them carried the news to the town,   230
that he had done what he had done.

As she sharpened her dulled talons,
the old woman said,
«What is it, what is it
my grandchild's husband has hold of?»

Her wings were like dry branches.
She flew low.
She flew there crookedly.
She teetered through the air.

There were five of them still above water   240
when she arrived.
When the last was just going under,
she grabbed hold.

After she flapped her wings for a time,
she started to pull them back up to the surface.
They came up in a line.
The thing he had hold of broke loose at the bottom.
He brought it up with him, they say.

They said, «Put it way, way out,
away from where people will go for their food.»   250

He took it way out to sea, they say.
Then he picked up a spring salmon and part
          of a humpback whale.
He flew back with them in his talons.
He had killed the thing that frightened them, they say.
It was a horseclam spirit being,[7] they say.

LATER ON, when he had lived with his wife for a while,   [5]
    he went to see his uncle's town, they say.
He flew there dressed in the skin of the eagle.
He perched for a while at the edge of the town,
and he saw his uncle come out of the house.   260
Then he flew away.

The next day, early, he flew there once again.
He picked up a humpback whale
and dropped it in front of his uncle's house
while the people were still sleeping.

Then he perched on a dead tree at the edge of town.
After a while, someone came out.
He called them to the whale, and they came.
His uncle claimed the whole thing for himself.
He stood up on top of the whale.   270

Then the eagle flew.
He flew around above his uncle.

They laughed at him.
«He is thinking of whale meat,»
they said.

And again he perched on the tree.
He sat there awhile,
and once again his uncle claimed the whale.
He stood there and declared it.

Then the eagle flew a second time.   280
He grabbed his uncle by his overgrown topknot[8]
and carried him away.

After he had carried him awhile,
his uncle knew the eagle was his nephew.
«Nephew!» he said,
«Take me back!
You'll be the one who marries my wife!
I will give you the town!»

After they had flown a little further,
he said the same thing to his nephew once again.   290
And after they had flown further still,
his nephew dropped him in the open sea.

Then he flew landward.
He went to his uncle's town.
There he married his uncle's wife.
He came to own the town, they say.
His uncle too became a spirit being in the open sea, they say.

So it ends.   298

Those Who Stay
a Long Way Out to Sea[1]

...AND THEN THERE WERE THE TEN OF THEM [1]
who went to hunt with dogs, they say.
And after they had travelled for a while,
the mist settled in.

And they came to a steep cliff,
and they climbed the cliff, they say.

And then their dogs ran back and forth on the ground below,
squawking up at them like gulls, they say.

And then they built a fire on top of the cliff.
The one they called the brainless one   10
fed his hunting bow to the fire, they say.
And after it had burned away completely,
it lay there in plain sight on the ground below.

Then he fed himself to the fire as well.
For a while he burned.
Then he vanished completely
and stood in plain sight on the ground below.
And he called to his elder brothers to do the same.

«Come on, do what I did.
I suffered no pain.»   20
So they started to feed themselves to the fire.

And one by one, as soon as they vanished,
they stood on the ground.

When they put in the next to the eldest,
his skin shrivelled up and his eyes bulged.
This was because he was frightened, they say.
But after he vanished,
he stood with the others below.

Then the eldest did the same.
That cliff is called The Tall Thin Rock, they say.   30

THEN they set off, they say.   [2]
    After they travelled a ways,
a wren sang to one side of them.
They could see that it punctured a blue hole
            through the heart
of the one who had passed closest to it, they say.

They went a ways further
and came to the head of Big Inlet,[2] they say.

And they went a ways further.
A falcon's feather floated there in front of them.
They tied it into the hair of the youngest, they say.   40
They tied it with skin from the throat of a mallard.
It made him look handsome.

Then they came to a seasonal village.
One house in the middle had roofplanks.
They stayed there, they say.
They gathered their food from the beds of blue mussels
            at one end of town.
And the brainless one played with the mussels.

He was trying to spit them as far as he could.
Soon the others were egging him on, they say.
One of them climbed up on top of the house   50
and held out his cape, away from his shoulder.

After a while he looked at the cape.
It was covered with feathers.
It is said they did not understand
that this was because they had broken their fast.

They walked through the town,
and they found an abandoned canoe, they say.
It was covered with moss.
Nettles grew over it too.

They cleaned it and patched it.   60
The brainless one made them a cedarbark bailer.
He carved a songbird perching on the handle.

Then they tied some feathers into another one's hair.
The brainless one got in the bow with a pole.
And one of them lay on his back in the stern.
They went down the inlet, they say.

A ND THEY WENT for a ways,   [3]
  and they came to a town
where a drum was sounding.
A shaman was calling his powers.   70

The firelight came through the doorway and all the way
        down to the shore.
They landed below it.

The bow man went up for a look,
and as he came near:
«Spirit Being Who Handles the Bow Pole is coming ashore!»

This made him embarrassed.
He returned to the canoe.

Another went up for a look,
and as he came near:
«Pierced by a Wren is coming ashore!»[3]   80
He looked at himself.
He was punctured and blue.
This made him embarrassed.
He backed away.

Another went up for a look,
and when he came near,
he also heard the shaman speaking.
«Now Spirit Being Who Holds up the Sky while He Travels
        is coming ashore!»
He went back too.

Then another went ashore,   90
and a voice said,
«Well now, Spirit Being Who Runs on the Water
        is coming ashore.»

Another went up for a look,
and when he came near:
«Here is Swimming Puffin Spirit coming ashore.»
He was embarrassed as well,
and he backed away.

Then the next one went ashore,
and a voice said,
«This is Falcon Feather Floating on the Water
        coming ashore!»   100
He took a close look at the shaman.
He saw that the shaman's clothes were the same as his own.
He went back too.

Yet another went ashore,
and when he came near:
«Well now, Necklace of Clouds is coming ashore!»
And he also backed off.

The next went ashore,
and as he came near:
«Now Spirit Being with Bulging Eyes is coming ashore!»   110
Then he remembered
that something had happened to him, they say.

Another went ashore.
When he came near the doorway:
«Well now, Spirit Being Who Lies on His Back on the Water
          is coming ashore.»
He went back to the canoe.

Then the eldest came up for a look,
and when he came near:
«Now Spirit Being Half of Whose Voice Is the Voice
          of the Raven,
who's in charge of the canoe, is coming ashore.»   120

And the eldest one said,
«It's true: we have turned into spirits.
If that's how it is,
we should be on our way.»

They took some of the village children aboard,
and they stuffed them into cracks in the hull of the canoe.
From one end of town, they gathered some grass
          to make nests.
They arranged it around themselves
where they were sitting.

THEN they headed for the open coast, they say.　　　130
　　When the one with the pole pushed them off,　　　[4]
the wood turned red wherever he touched it.
He moved the canoe by himself with only the pole.

As they travelled along,
they found feathers afloat on the sea.
They put them in a painted box and saved them.
Flicker feathers were their favourite,
and they saved them above all.

They came to another town,
and they beached the canoe.　　　140
Not far away, a woman was crying.
They brought her aboard.

When this woman's husband came in from his fishing,
he saw someone's arms embracing his wife.
He threw live coals on the hands,
but his wife was the only one there,
and the only one screaming.

She is the one who was sitting there crying.
They took her aboard, they say.

They opened the cracks in the hull,　　　150
and they stuffed in her hands.
That cured her, they say.
They adopted her as their sister
and gave her the seat reserved for the bailer.

THEN, they say, they arrived off Qaysun,　　　[5]
　　and Fairweather Woman, the headwater woman
　　　　of Swiftcurrent Creek, came out to meet them.
«Hello, my brothers. I'll give you directions.
The eldest brother sits amidships.

He's in charge of the canoe.
His name will be Spirit Half of Whose Voice
      Is the Voice of the Raven.   160

«Half the canoe should be Eagle
  and half of it Raven.
  Half of the dancing hats should be black
  and half of them white.

«Next will be the one whose name is Spirit Being
        with Bulging Eyes.
  Next will be Pierced by a Wren.[4]
  Next, Spirit Being Who Holds up the Sky while He Travels.
  Next, Spirit Being Who Runs on the Water.
  Next, the one named Swimming Puffin Spirit Being.
  Next, the one called Necklace of Clouds.   170
  Next, Spirit Being Who Lies on His Back on the Water.
  Next, Spirit Being Who Handles the Bow Pole.
  He will set the course of the canoe.
  He will take you wherever you go
  to give power to people.
  And the next to the youngest will be Falcon Feather
        Floating on the Water.

«Your sister, who sits in the stern,
  will be called Spirit Woman Who Keeps Bailing.

«Now, my brothers, take your seats in the canoe.
  Go to Charcoal Island.   180
  He's the one who paints the spirit beings.
  He will paint you.

«For four nights you will dance in your canoe.
  Then you will be finished with your changing.»

Four years is what she meant, they say.

That one also gave them clothes.
He dressed them in dancing hats and aprons
    with puffin-beak rattles.
Then he wrapped a skin of cloud around the whole canoe.
Inside the cloud, he assigned them their seats
and built them the nests that they sit on.[5]   190

Then it was finished.

This is where it ends.

Hlagwajiina and His Family[1]

H

IS WIFE AND HE WERE THE ONLY TWO   [1.1]
     in town, they say.
A lamprey spirit had killed the rest of the people.
A big dog remained with them as well.

Her husband went out fishing,
and as usual, they say, he worked the halibut banks
       just in front of the village.
As soon as he left, his wife went out to dig spruce roots.
The dog tagged along with her, they say.

When her husband came to shore,
she steamed him a halibut
and piled it onto a platter.   10

He sat up high,
and when he started eating,
his wife looked out the door.
Watching him frightened her.
She also looked away when her husband went out fishing.

O

NCE, as she was digging spruce roots,   [1.2]
     right between the thighs, something surprised her.
She looked behind her.
Sure enough, the dog had got her.
She cried for quite a while.   20

Then her husband came in from his fishing again,
and she cooked for him
and set the food before him
and turned away as always, toward the door.
Soon she knew she was pregnant, they say.

And one day, while her husband was out fishing,
she gave birth, they say.
She gave birth to a dog.
And then to another, and then to another,
and so on, until there were nine. 30

The middle one of the litter kept showing his teeth.
That was the brave one, they say.
The youngest was born chewing leaves.
Then, at the end, came a female puppy.
There were ten of them in all.

She didn't have the heart to kill them.
She put grass in the cellar
and put them in there.

When her husband came home,
she avoided his eyes. 40

ON THE FOLLOWING DAY, her husband [1.3.1]
  went fishing again,
and she went to dig spruce roots.

The moment she left the house,
there was noise from inside it.
They had already started to challenge each other.
The female's voice was the sharpest.

She went back to the house.
She peeked through a crack at the edge of the doorflap.

Their skins were hanging on pegs in back of the fire.
They were playing their game in another part of the house.   50

When she rustled the doorflap,
they raced for their skins.
Moments later they lay in a row at the edge of the fire.
She put them back into the cellar.

Her husband came in.
«My child's mother,» he said to her,
«what was the noise that came from the town?»

«The dog was chasing his tail.
and rattled the floorplanks.»

THE FOLLOWING DAY, as soon as her husband   [1.3.2]
went fishing again,   60
she went out to get roots.
And as soon as she left, there was noise in the house.

This time she didn't go back so soon.
She gathered a pile of dry firewood.
Then she peeked in.

Their skins once again hung on pegs in the back of the house.
When she rattled the doorflap again,
they ran back to the skins and retrieved them
and curled up at the edge of the fire.
Then she put them back into the cellar.   70

When Hlagwajiina came ashore,
he asked again, «My child's mother,
what was all that noise that came from town?»

«The dog was playing with himself
and kept shaking the floorplanks.»

WHEN he went out fishing again, [1.3.3]
    the dog lay sprawled at one side of the fire.
She threw a rock in his direction.
«What sort of creature won't even get wood
    for the one who has borne him his children?» 80

Then he got up.
He shook his whole body.
Then he went out.

A noise came from in back of the house
and she peered through a gap in the houseplanks.
Someone with amulets dangling all the way down
            to his thighs from a giant topknot,
                    and stripes on his skin,
sauntered along with the trunk of a dry tree.

After the noise had gone on for a while,
the dog came inside.
He shook and lay down at one side of the fire. 90

Her husband came ashore and said,
«Where did you get all this nice, dry firewood?»

«From a windfall tree I brought out of the forest.»

THE FOLLOWING DAY, he went fishing again, [1.3.4]
    and his wife went out again to dig for spruce roots.

Before she went out, she put wood on the fire.
As soon as she left, they were back in the house,
            making a racket.
Then she moved quietly.

She had left the doorflap half open, they say.

When she looked inside,   100
their skins were hanging, again, in the rear of the house.

They had started a wrestling match with each other.
After she watched them awhile,
they wrestled each other into a corner.

She raced inside, they say.
She grabbed the skins and threw them in the fire.
The skins disappeared,
and the children stood there, facing her over the fire.
One of them was a girl.

Then she said to them,   110
«My darlings, when your father comes in and has dinner,
don't ever look at him.
I will feed you after he has eaten.
No one ever looks him in the face.»

T HE one named Sawahliixha ran outside.   [1.3.5]
Hlagwajiina was anchored offshore.
«Huu! Huuuuu! Huu!» he hollered.
The more his mother shushed him,
the more he carried on.

Hlagwajiina came ashore,   120
and his wife steamed fish for him as usual.
After she had set the food before him,
she turned and faced the door.

Before Hlagwajiina had eaten his meal,
Sawahliixha stood up.
He picked up a fat piece of the bellyflesh of the fish
and stood there eating.

After he ate it,
he picked up another.
After he ate it,   130
he gave the tray a shove.

H LAGWAJIINA called his wife.   [1.4]
  «My child's mother, bring me my cape.»
She brought it out,
and then he put it on.

He summoned the eldest.
«Dear boy, let me sing you a song.»
He went to him.

When he had sung to him awhile,
he pulled him closer to his breast.   140
It was as if he went to sleep.
«My child has fallen asleep.
He must be tired.»

He summoned another.
That one went to him as well,
and after he had sung to him awhile,
he pulled him to his breast.
It was the same with him:
«My child has fallen asleep.»

He did the same with eight of them.   150
After that he called the youngest boy,
the one who chewed the leaves.

When he had sung to him awhile
and pulled him close,
the child spat his medicine at Hlagwajiina's chest.
Sharp spines fell from him in splinters
and stood sticking in the floorplanks.

Hlagwajiina turned his garment back to front.
He sang the boy another song,
and then he pulled him close.   160
Again the child spat his medicine at Hlagwajiina's chest.
The spines fell off from there as well.

He lost his temper then, they say,
and went after him in earnest.
He shoved him toward the whetstone
that stood up on edge in the rear of the house.

As he touched it,
it rubbed away his thigh.
He spat the medicine into his hands
and smeared it on his body   170
and became the same as he had been before.

When they had struggled there awhile,
he threw his father down, they say.
He fell against the whetstone.
He ground away to nothing.
The child let the whetstone kill his father.

H E WENT to where his elder brothers lay   [1.5]
and set them side by side
and spat the medicine upon them.
They twitched and sat up.   180
«We must have drifted off.»

They kept the shapes they had
and kept on living in the house.

These are some of their names.
The eldest was called Ghuusghadliikka, which means
       the One Who Didn't Know How to Turn into Stone.

Another was called Gustalaana, Lefthanded.
He was fearless, they say.

Sawahliixha was the heedless one.
Another was called Hlghangaaʻu.
Tlaaganaaqati was the one who chewed the leaves.[2]   190

　　　　　⟩　　　⟩　　　⟩

AND THEN, they say, they asked their mother,   [2.1]
　　«Mother, why is the village so empty?»

«My darling, one of the spirit beings
　who live at the toe of the island
　got rid of your uncles.
　The town has been empty like this ever since.»

Then, they say, they talked to one another.
«Let's go see it tomorrow.»

Next morning they did go to see it, they say.
It lived in a cave.
Human bones were piled up in front of it.   200
They looked at it,
and then they went away.

THEN they put something together in order to kill it.   [2.2]
　The nine boys started twisting cedar limbs.
They twined the strands together right away,
and right away they spliced them end to end.
They made it long.
They made it thick.

The next day, they went after it, they say.
When they came to where it was,   210
they grabbed their sister by the neck
and strung her up on the end of a pole.

They used her as bait.

They set the snare in front of its den.
After they dangled their sister there in front of it awhile,
it started to move.
They pulled her back before it as it came.

When it was halfway out of its cave
and straddled the loop of the snare,
they sprang the trap.   220

They pulled their sister back at the same time
and spat the medicine upon her.
She started pulling alongside them on the far end of the line.

When it had dragged out all their line
and started to pull them into a heap,
the rope snapped,
and all of them tumbled backward.
Then they went away, they say.

AFTER brooding on the problem for a while,   [2.3]
they decided to go and dig spruce roots, they say.   230
They prowled around on Ghasqw Island.³
They got the roots from there.
Then they spliced these too.

When their spruceroot rope was long enough,
they went to it again.
Again they used their sister as the lure.
Again they set the snare in front of it.

After it emerged,
they pulled the snare taut at the midpoint of its body.
Again they pulled their sister back   240
and spat the medicine upon her.

Again she grabbed the far end of the snare.

After it had pulled them down repeatedly,
the rope broke.
They fell head over heels.
Then they went away again, they say.

T HEN they took the long stipes of seaweed   [2.4]
          that lay there high and dry.
They moved around the island, gathering them up.
Right away they stretched them out.
Right away they spliced them.   250

When it was long enough,
they went to it again.
Again they used their sister as bait.
When that broke too,
they gave it up, they say.
There was nothing they could use.

W HEN they had gone on living there awhile,   [2.5]
          a wren chirped in the corner of the house.
How about sinew, my sinew, my sinew, my sinew?
          it seemed to keep saying.

They brooded on its words,   260
and they all made bows and blunt-tipped arrows.
Then they prowled around the island.
They came back frequently with three or four birds each.

Their sister pulled the sinews out at once.
At once they twisted them together.
It was thin!

When it was long enough,
they went there once again, they say.

They rigged the snare.
Again they baited the pole with their sister.   270
Again, as he came out, they tripped the snare.

They jerked their sister back at once
and spat the medicine upon her.
Right away she started pulling alongside them.
They pulled on it hard.
It stretched even thinner.

When they pulled it across the face of the cliff,
the rock broke off.
«Yes! With the sinews of wrens!» they kept saying.

When they had pulled for quite a while,   280
a cracking sound came from the base of the island.
Then they pulled it up.
They slit its belly open.
Out through the slit came human bones.

They laid the bones together.
Wherever one was missing,
they broke up twigs and branches
and put them in instead.
Tlaaganaaqati spat the medicine upon them right away.

«Go back to where you used to live,» they said.   290

They had killed it,
and they went away, they say.
It was a lamprey spirit being, they say.

        ➤   ➤   ➤

WHEN they had lived awhile longer   [3.1.1]
     in the same place,
their sister entered womanhood, they say.

One night, a while later, there was someone
        speaking sweetly to their sister.
None of them knew who it was that was speaking.

The next night, there was someone speaking sweetly
        with their sister once again.
They put some spruce gum on the mat, they say.

That night again, there was someone speaking sweetly
        with their sister.   300

Next day at dawn, they went into the sea to bathe
        as they did every winter morning.
Coming back, they saw patches of gum
        on the thigh of the heedless one.
They shoved him from one to another.
They laughed at him.

Then, they say, their mother said,
«It seems they laugh
   because the Child of Fast Water's severed head is soon to hang
   before their sister in her puberty seclusion.»

RIGHT AWAY they went to ask an old man   [3.1.2]
        living at the edge of town
to tell them what to do, they say.   310
They asked about the thing their mother mentioned.

They gave him some cedar-limb line.
Along with that, they gave him bones
for making marlinspikes, they say,
and Haida tobacco besides.

He told them where the one they asked for could be found.
He told them that he slept right where he stood,
and he told them he was easy to get close to.

134

They went at once to borrow someone's fast canoe.

T HEY BORROWED the canoe   [3.1.3]
    of The One Who Outruns Trout.[4]   320
He stood amidships,
and while all of them were paddling as one,
he shot an arrow toward the bow.
It landed just amidships, to one side of the canoe.

Then they borrowed Steelhead's canoe.
He also shot an arrow
as all of them paddled.
It landed at the stern of the canoe.
In spite of that, they thought it was too slow.

They also borrowed one from Jellyfish.[5]   330
His boat had a stern at either end.
They could launch it either way.
It wasn't pretty,
but they borrowed it.

«I'm coming with you,» said the Jellyfish, they say.
They singed the bottom of the hull.
They launched the boat, they say.

That one stood amidships
and reached his tentacles to seaward.
He shot an arrow forward as they paddled.   340
It landed far back in their wake.

Then they brought the boat up on the beach,
and then they got ready to go on their journey, they say.

O NE DAY the sea and sky were calm and fair.   [3.1.4]
    They went to talk to the old man.
They say he was the Heron.

«It's a fine morning.»
«No, my lords,» he said, «the day is foul.»

Another day it was foggy in the morning.
Mist lay close upon the water.   350
They went to see him anyway.
He was sitting outside.

«Launch the canoe.
It's a beautiful morning,» he said.
«When it gets to be noon, the sun will come through.»

Then he told them what to do.
«When he sleeps, there is light in his eyes.
Paddle close to him then.
When you don't see a light in his eyes, stay away.»

Then they put to sea, they say.   360

WHEN they had paddled for a while,   [3.1.5]
     they saw his shining eyes.
They had skookum root[6] soaking in aged urine, they say.
They gathered up the strands of floating hair.[7]
After that, they cut his head off, they say.

The Jellyfish stretched his tentacles to landward.
They worked their paddles once again.
Their bow-wake split a fissure in the sea.
That's where they poured out the skookum root and the urine.

Their stern-wake cracked the sea as well.   370
They poured the mixture there as well.
Then they arrived in front of the town.

Right away they suspended the head in front of their sister.
It had long flowing hair.

N EXT DAY a being came singing out of the sea.   [3.2.1]
    He carried a staff.
It was red.
He came out of the water in front of the town.
«Give me my son's head!» he said.
«Or else I'll flip your village upside down.»   380

Two of them ran to the old one, they say.
«Old man! What shall we do?
    He says he'll flip the village upside down!»

«Start at one side of town
    and pile white agates on top of it.
    Cover the village from bottom to top.»

They ran back at once
    and did as he told them, they say.

Then that one said to them again,
«Give me my son's head!   390
    Or else I'll flip your village upside down.»
    Then Sawahliixha said,
«So go ahead and flip it.»

He struck one end of town with the red stick in his hand.
It just quivered.
He did it from one side of town to the other.
It just shuddered and shook.

Then he gave it up
    and moved offshore.
He vanished into the ocean.   400

N EXT DAY again he came   [3.2.2]
    singing songs without words.
Small red beings flocked behind him.

Those, they say, were beach-fleas.

They rushed to the old man
and they asked him for advice.
«What shall we do?»

«Boil some urine
and fling it in their direction.»
They started to boil it.

«My son's head!»   410

At that moment the beach-fleas swarmed toward the house,
and they hurled the urine in their direction.
After they had killed off half of them,
he went back out to sea.
He vanished into the ocean.

N EXT DAY he came again.   [3.2.3]
  A flock of creatures was flying behind him.
They were siskins, they say.[8]

Again they asked the old man what to do.
He said to make blunt-headed arrows.   420
They did so.

As soon as he said «My son's head!»
the birds swarmed toward the house.
They went toward them and shot them.
After they had killed off half of them,
he moved offshore again.

N EXT DAY again he was there   [3.2.4]
  singing songs without words.
Behind him the skin of the rolling ocean was burning.
They ran to the old man again right away.

«Now, my lords, there is nothing whatsoever to be done.   430
Get away while you can.»
That's what he told them.

THEY RAN OFF at once, they say, taking the head.   [3.2.5]
    The earth went up in flames behind them.
As one of them caught fire,
he tossed it to another.
Soon the only one left was the one who chewed medicine.

One side of his body caught fire,
and he rubbed himself with the medicine
and made himself the way he was before.   440

After a while he flung what he was holding toward the flames.
The fire stopped there,
and then it receded.

THEN he walked all around there,   [3.3]
    looking for the places
        where his brothers had been burned.
There was no sign of their bones.

After he had walked along awhile,
he called out to the heedless one.
«Sawahliixhaaaaaaaaaa!»

«Here.»   450

He went to where the voice was.
Their bones were all together in a heap.
He spat the medicine on them.

They twitched and sat up.
«We must have drifted off,» they said.

Then, they say, they headed back
    toward the boundary between worlds.[9]

Then they rebuilt their house,
which had burned to the ground.
They restored their sister and mother to life,
and they lived there again.[10]   460

            ❧   ❧   ❧

O NE DAY, later on, they heard the sound   [4.1]
    of someone talking to their sister.
There was someone in bed with their sister.
The North Wind is who it was, they say.

He came out and sat by the fire
but he never let his other side get warm.

The heedless one thought about this
and started to whittle a pile of shavings.
He dried them.
Some of the shavings came from pitchwood.
Those he mixed in with the others.   470

One day at dawn, his sister's lover came out by the fire.
He sat above the fire.
The heedless one also came and sat above the fire.
Then he tossed the shavings in the flames.

When the fire blazed up,
their sister's lover jumped back.
Ho! His cock went *whap!* against his belly,
and they laughed at him.

Then he said,
«You're making fun of me.   480
I'll fight you.»

The day after that, he departed, they say.

He swelled up fat and black at the head of the Stikine.
Snow fell from him.
One of them went out to see what he looked like, they say.
He didn't return.

Then another one went out to see what he looked like.
He never returned.
It continued this way
until all of them vanished.   490

Still, the one who chewed the medicine remained.
Then he also went out to see what he looked like, they say.
As he travelled along,
he saw that his brothers were frozen.

Ice started sticking to him too.
Then he licked himself with medicine,
and all the ice fell off.
He went directly toward the big, black cloud.
And then he arrived.

Ice was spewing out of that one's bum.   500
This one kissed the tips of his arrows with medicine
and shot the arrows at the ice.

He leapt aside,
and an avalanche landed
where he had been standing.
He did this again and again,
and then he headed back, they say.

As he went back along the trail,
he chewed the healing leaves and spat
        toward the frozen bodies of his brothers.   510

They joined him right away.
They travelled all together.

AFTER they had travelled for a while   [4.2]
    they came to someone's dwelling place, they say.
He gave them food, of course,
and then they stayed the night.

Sawahliixha woke up.
Their host lay in bed in one corner.

Then that one got up
and tied cedarbark wool   520
to the tip of a stick that hung over his bed.
He went round with it, holding it out
where [each of the sleepers] would breathe on it.

Then he took it outside.
Sawahliixha went out on his heels.

Under a waterfall was a redcedar lid.
He lifted it up
and poked in the cedarbark wool.

Sawahliixha was watching.
Then Sawahliixha came back to the house   530
and lay down, as though he were sleeping.

Soon that one came back and lay down.
Then this one held cedarbark wool where that one
            would breathe on it.
Then he went out.

Sawahliixha pulled out the cedarbark wool
that that one pushed in
and pushed his in instead.

Then he went back and lay down.

Next day, after that one had fed them,
he bathed.   540
Then he began to feel poorly, they say.

He said his chest and head were sick.
«I must have done it to myself.»
He died soon after that, they say.
That was the spirit being Put Yourself to Sleep, they say.

Then they continued their journey, they say.
They all came home.

L ATER ON, they headed out again, they say.   [4.3]
      They hunted birds.
Then one of them went missing.   550
It continued like this
until they were gone.

The one who chewed the leaves remained alone, they say.
He followed the tracks of his brothers.

He found his brothers perched on a snag
and did not understand
how they got there, they say.
Be that as it may, he was perched up there with them.

High in the air, they broke up their bows and their arrows.
They kindled a fire.
After the weapons had burned completely away,   560
they appeared in one piece on the ground below.

Then each of them put himself into the fire
and each reappeared on the ground below.
The North Wind was the cause of this, they say.

And then they all went back, they say.
They arrived at the place where they lived.

ʼ ʼ ʼ

L ATER ON, when they had moved around awhile,   [5.1.1]
  they came to Marmot's Peak, they say.
They built themselves a house there.
Then they built deadfalls.   570

The cold weather came,
and they kept going out on the trapline, they say.
They made marmot-skin britches, they say.

When they went out again,
the second youngest found no marmots in his traps, they say.
He didn't get a one.

Then, when they started for home,
he refused to go with them, they say.

They gave him two each.
He refused them.   580
They offered him five.
He refused them again,
and they started for home without him, they say.

O NE NIGHT, after he'd lived there alone for a while,   [5.1.2]
  a woman came and lay down beside him, they say.
He made love to her.

Then she asked him a question.
«Why don't you get any game in your deadfalls?»

«Whatever I do, I get none,» he replied.

«Set ten deadfalls tomorrow.»   590

Next day, he did so.
The day after that, he went out on the trapline.
Ten marmots were there for him.

hen he had done this for a time,
and had caught a great many,
he was checking his trapline one morning.
A white one ran into a burrow in front of his eyes.
His wife warned him not to trap that one.

It was all he could think of.
He set up a trap right in front of its burrow.   600
He caught it the very next day.
Then he thought of his wife,
and he hung it outside of the house, they say.

Without leaving her seat, his wife felt it happen.
«My mother is crying *Aiiiii! My child!*»

She packed up her things at that moment, they say.
He tried to persuade her to stay.
He made no impression at all.

She paused in the doorway
and called,   610
«Come to life!»

They were suddenly swarming around.
Then he tried to club them
and to trap them with the door.
He had no effect on them either.

And then he went with them, they say.

When he had been chasing his wife for a ways,
she dived into a burrow.

He dived into it also, they say.

There also they lived as husband and wife.   620
They harvested a lot of different things,
        including nettle roots.

W HEN the snow began to fall,   [5.1.3]
        they went to bed, they say.
They slept,
and after they had slept for quite some time,
the morning came.

Then he stood at the doorway,
calling, «It's morrrrrning!»
They jumped out of bed,
wearing nothing.   630

«Where is it morning?
Has morning come up to the nettle roots?»
they asked one another.
They looked at the snow,
and they went back to bed.

After doing this twice,
he gave up
and stayed in his bed.

L ATER ON, when the snow disappeared,   [5.1.4]
        they put on their skins   640
and started to harvest the nettle roots.
He went with them again.

Later, they say, one of them hollered,
«Humans are coming!»
Then they went into their houses.

Again, the others set deadfalls.
There were marmot designs on the posts of the deadfalls,
     they say.
All the marmots could see were the shadows of hands.
The designs were to call them, they say.

One went out for a look   650
and was caught in a trap.
The hunters took him
while the marmots watched from their house.

He wanted to go,
but his wife held him back.

L ATER ON, he went out   [5.1.5]
   and was caught in a deadfall, they say.
The hunters took him to their house
and hung him up.

As one of them started to skin him,   660
making his first cut from the throat,
he struck something hard.

When they looked,
they saw – yes! – the necklace of copper
worn by the brother who'd stayed in that place.

They discussed it,
and then they put some of their brother's own clothes
     over top of him.
After they smeared him with medicine,
he sat up, they say.

«I must have drifted off,»   670
he said as he woke.
His brothers were happy to see him.

Then he left with them, they say.
They went to live yet again in their own house.

LATER ON, when they had moved around awhile,   [5.2]
    the eldest disappeared again, they say.
The next day another disappeared.
One went out to track him
and he also disappeared.

After a time, no one was left except the one
            who chewed the medicine.   680
Then he took his bow
and followed his brothers' tracks from the side of the house.

After he had walked a little ways,
he came upon a feather floating overhead.
Then he was yanked off his feet by a snare.
He hung in mid-air.
He started to faint,
and he smeared his neck with the medicine.

At dawn the next day,
someone with paint on his face arrived on the inland trail.   690
«My snare has been lucky again!»

After that one cut him down,
he heard him talking to his snare.
«Don't let anything go past,» he told it.

And this one thought,
«If only he would carry me face up.»
And that one grabbed him by the legs
and carried him face up.

When that one ducked beneath a windfall,
this one grabbed it.   700

After that one tugged awhile,
this one lost his grip.

Soon they came to that one's house,
and that one plunked him down inside.
His elder brothers had been butchered
and hung up to dry in the rear of the house.

While that one slept,
this one gathered up the corpses of his brothers
and carried them outside.

After walking for a while,   710
he noticed they were missing.
He'd forgotten all about the healing leaves he chewed,
        they say.
Then he went back
and smeared them all with medicine.

They came to life,
and they set off with him, they say.
And the next day, they arrived once again at their village.

T HEN they headed out again.   [5.3]
    When they had moved around awhile,
the one who chewed the medicine lost track of them.   720

After he had searched for them awhile,
he came upon a being
using his own skull for a drum.

«Did my elder brothers pass this way?» he asked.

«Did my elder brothers pass this way?»
the other one replied.

«Act like that
and I might kill you.»
Then the other said the very same.

«If that's the way you act,   730
I'll take your head!»
Again the other said the same.

That was Echo Spirit Being, they say.
No matter what he said,
he could get nothing different for an answer.

Then, when he said that he would fart at him,
the other lost his nerve.
«Anything but that, sir! Anything but that!»

When he did blow a fart at him,
the other disappeared, they say.   740
This one made him vanish just like that, they say.

After he had looked still further for his brothers,
he came upon a big, wide, slippery slab of stone
          with feathers on the top.
There beside it lay his brothers' bones.
All of them had died, they say,
while trying to pluck feathers from the stone.

Again he spat the healing leaves upon his brothers.
Then they all woke up, they say.

WHEN they had travelled and travelled some more,   [5.4]
    they came to a place   750
where a woman was living.
In the usual way, she offered them all kinds of food.
Her serving dish was carved in the form of a mouse.

They planned to sleep there at her camp, they say.
But the house was full of scratching sounds all night.
They couldn't sleep.

They left before the night was through, they say,
and came back to the house
where their mother and sister were living.[11]

THEN they got ready to go again,   760
and they spoke to their mother.   [5.5]
«Make this place your own.
This is the last we will see of you.»
They told their sister to come with them.

They went way up the Stikine River then, they say.
And before they started swimming across,
though it had been ten years
since their sister entered womanhood,
they told her not to watch them as they swam.

They locked arms with each other   770
and they swam across, they say.
The one who chewed medicine was the last to enter the water.
And they turned into rocks
when their sister looked up at them.[12]

Their elder brother sang for a bit,
looking back at them.
He composed the song that goes
Not even Tlaaganaaqati could make it across.
That is the place they are living, they say.[13]

And this is the place where it stops.   780

The Names of Their Gambling Sticks[1]

H IS FATHER WAS A RICH MAN   [1]
       at Sea Lion Village, they say.
His father's name was Poor Man's Son.
And his father was ready to sponsor a potlatch, they say.
His father went over himself to invite the Tsimshian, they say.
While his father was gone, Gasinanju started
       to gamble, they say.

After gambling awhile,
he had lost his father's property.
Then he put a gutsack full of oil into his gambling bag,
       they say.
He slung it on his back,
and then he left, they say.   10

A FTER walking for a time,   [2]
    he turned and went toward Whiterock.
He ate every sort of medicine he found.

Soon the diarrhea came.
Sitting on a windfall, he let loose, they say.
Moving on, he continued eating leaves.

After walking on a ways,
they say he came across the moss-coated bones
       of a pair of human beings.

After walking further still,
he came to where a pair of creeks pours down steeply
      from Juujitga.[2]   20
The bones of two more humans – fresh, they say –
      were resting on the bank.

One creek was red.
The other creek was blue.
Juujitga's shit made this one red, they say.
His medicine, they say, made that one blue.
Those who drink the reddened water die right there, they say.

He drank the oil from his bag
and coated his insides with it, they say.
Then he knelt by the blue stream.
After just a few sips,   30
he lost all sense of where he was.

WHEN he came to himself,   [3]
    a large house with a two-headed housepole
stood just in front of him.
They asked him in.
He went through the door right away.

«The birds are singing about you, grandson,»
said the headman of the house.
«You gambled away what your father was going to give.»

The headman had a small box brought to him.   40
He lifted out a blue falcon's feather
and slipped it into the corner of the young man's eye.
When he had wiggled it around and pulled it out,
he showed him blood and moss.

After cleaning both his eyes,
the headman said, «Let me see your gambling sticks.»

Gasinanju handed them over.
The other one squeezed them, they say.
Blood came out of them as well.

After he had held his fingers to his lips,   50
he ran the tip of his finger around the middle of one
        of the sticks.
Where he touched it, it turned red.
«This one's name,» he said, «will be *Ten in a Row.*»

After touching his lips with his fingers again,
he pressed the tips of another stick with his fingers.
The tips turned red, they say.
«This one,» he said, «will be known as *Poking the Clouds.*»

As he handed back the sticks,
he called them by their names.
Shifting Riches, Flying Far, Whale Blubber,   60
Starting for Shore, Little Plain One, Noisy Bones,
and *Hermit Thrush* are the names that he gave them.[3]

In the corner of the house lay a heap of big canoes.
This is because the Tsimshian had lifted their prows
clear of the tide in the place Gasinanju had come from,
        they say.

Two transparent boys were in the headman's house.
One of them was going to go back with him,
the headman said.

«This one will go with you.
He will pull the trump stick from your pack   70
whenever it's your turn to work the sticks.[4]

«Never pick the smoking cedarbark.
Take the one that doesn't smoke.

When your score is six,
pick the smoking one instead.
Then get ready with *Ten in a Row*.»

After he had told him this,
he said to him, «It's time for you to leave.»
Gasinanju woke as though he'd been sleeping.

H E W E N T away the same way he had come, they say.   80
   Out beyond the windfall where he stopped   [4]
      to take a crap on the way up,
an old sea otter lolled.
He studied the sea.
The otter was drifting to shore.

He went out to it and got it.
He dried the hide.
Then he went back to Sea Lion Village.

Just before he got there,
he came across some dogs
who were fighting over a gambling bag   90
where a broad red trail came out on the left.
Tallow in the bag is what the dogs were after.

He picked it up.
In the bottom of the bag was a little copper shield.
He took it with him to the village.

He came to the ten canoes
that the Tsimshian had lifted up above the tideline.
He went to see his mother.
He was careful what he ate.
He drank a lot of water too.   100

NEXT MORNING, they tell me, the gambling   [5.1]
     got underway.
He wagered the pelt.
The Tsimshian vied with one another
for the privilege of polishing him off.
Then one of them came out to start to gamble.

The Tsimshian was the first to work the sticks.
Gasinanju kept on picking out the bark that didn't smoke.
When his score was six,
he picked the bark that smoked instead.
He got the trump.   110

Then, they say, he got ready with *Ten in a Row*,
the way he'd been told.
«It's just as he said,» he kept saying.

It was his turn to work the sticks.
He got to ten.
His trump lay hidden with *Poking the Clouds*, they say.
It was going his way.
He stopped losing.

He worked the sticks again.
As he shuffled the pack,   120
he kept pushing the trump to one side of the pile, they say.
Someone took it away.
Again and again, they saw nothing.

He won everything from the Tsimshian.
When they had nothing left to lose,
he also won their ten canoes, they tell me.

A FTER a bit, a little old man in back of the crowd   [5.2]
       on the other side,
who had bathed and painted the right side of his face,
came up to gamble, they say.

When they had discussed the stakes for a while,   130
the Tsimshian worked the sticks.
Both heaps of cedarbark smoked.
He chose the one that smoked the most.
It was a loser.

The Tsimshian worked the sticks again.
He chose the one that smoked the least.
It too was a loser.

It was this Tsimshian's lucky day, they tell me.
That's why Gasinanju couldn't see his trump.
None of the others could beat him, they say.   140

A ND THE RICHES flowed at his father's potlatch,   [5.3]
       they tell me.
They gave the Tsimshian back their canoes.
And his father tattooed the breast of his son, they tell me.

He drew the form of a Cormorant on his body.
He put it right through him.
He spread out the wings so they covered both
       of his shoulders.
He put the beak of the bird on his chest,
and down his back he put its tail.

Never before had a Cormorant stood
for someone on the Raven side, they say.
No one did it this way later either, they tell me.

And the Tsimshian went seaward, they tell me.   150

       ➤   ➤   ➤

H<small>E MADE</small> the housepole of his father's house   [*Coda*]
      the same as Juujitga's, they tell me.
They named the house Two-Headed House, they tell me.
This is why The Ones Who Paddle Seaward have their own
      names for their gambling sticks, they tell me.[5]

A Red Feather[1]

T HE CHILDREN OF THE VILLAGE took their sticks   [1]
          and whacked a pine-burl puck
                    back and forth relentlessly, they tell me.
After they had played the game awhile,
they hollered *score! score! score!*, they say.

The niece of the mother of the town
was just becoming a woman, they tell me.[2]
She was sitting by herself behind the screens.

After the game had gone on for a while,
a red feather floated overhead, they say.
A while after that, they say, a child grabbed the feather.
It stuck to his fingers.
It lifted him up and carried him off.   10

Someone grabbed him by the feet.
When he was lifted up as well,
another grabbed his feet,
and this continued until everyone in town
was lifted in a string and carried off, they say.

The one becoming a woman there in the house
no longer heard their voices.
She was puzzled.

She peeked out.
There was no one in the house.

She went outside.   20
There was no one in the village.
She entered all the houses, one by one.
She saw that every one of them was empty.

She started to weep as she walked through the town.
She tied her robe up tight.
Then she blew her nose
and wiped the snot beneath her arm.

She got some woodchips
that her brothers had been playing with
and put them into the inner folds of her clothes.   30
She put birds' down, a crabapple twig, cedarbark strips,
        and dirt from a spot that her brothers had walked on
into the inner folds of her clothes along with the woodchips.

A FTER A TIME, without knowing a man,   [2]
     she was pregnant, they say.
She gave birth very quickly, they say.

She conceived again.
And again she gave birth to a boy.
This continued to happen.

The youngest was born with leaves in his mouth
and a blue hole in his cheek.   40
There were ten children including a girl, they say.
And she started to raise them, they say.

She brought into the house
all the food that was stored in the town.
She fed her children with this.

Soon they grew larger.
They played in the house.

A FTER A TIME, they say, one of them asked,   [3]
   «Mother, whose village is sitting here empty?»
«My darling,» said his mother, «this is the town
     of my brothers, your uncles.»   50
Then she told them the story.

«Day after day, the children of this village played
     with pucks and sticks.
Then a red feather floated in the air above their heads.
I was sitting underneath the floorplanks.
I conceived you and bore you here in an empty village
when I was the only one left.»

That's what she told them, they say.

Then he asked his mother what she meant by
playing with pucks and sticks.

«They made a gnarled burl nice and smooth,» she said,
and then they whacked it back and forth with sticks.»   60

They went to hunt for one at once, they say.
They made the things,
and after they were made,
they played with them there on the tiers of the housefloor.
They were still there playing when daylight came.

Next day, they moved the game outside.
The feather floated there above them, as before.
Their mother instructed them not to take hold
     of the feather, they say.

After the game had gone on for a while,
the eldest, who was reckless,   70
reached for the feather, they say.

It stuck to his fingers,
but just as it lifted him up,
he turned into snot.

When he had stretched out five times taller than he was,
he was lifted off his feet, they say.

Another one grabbed hold.
He turned into woodchips.
After he was lifted from the ground five times,
he too was pulled away.   80

Another one grabbed hold.
He turned into birds' down.
He unfolded into five as he was lifted from the ground.
Then he was pulled up too.

Yet another one grabbed hold.
He turned into cedarbark strips.
When he uncoiled to be five times taller than he was,
he too was pulled away.

Another one grabbed hold,
and that one turned to mud.   90
When he had stretched out five times taller than he was,
he was also pulled away.

Then another one grabbed hold.
After this had happened again and again,
nearly all of them were gone, they say.

And then, when another one grabbed hold,
he was changed to a crabapple tree.
He was strong, they say.

As it was pulling him and stretching him,
his sister danced around him.   100
She sharpened her nails, they say.
She kept telling her brother,
«Be tough! Be a genuine man!»

When just one of his roots remained in the ground,
his sister started climbing up, they say.
When she had climbed up to the feather
and had slashed at it awhile,
she cut it free, they say.

The string of them fell to the ground,
and the one who had leaves in his mouth   110
straddled his elder brothers.
He spat the medicine on all his elder brothers.
Then they stood up.

The bones of the others pulled up in a string from the village
were lying there too.
He also spat the medicine on them,
and they stood up as well.
Suddenly the town was repeopled, they say.

T HEY CONTINUED to play with the feather, they say.   [4]
 They waved it around through the town.   120

A while later, snow started falling, they say.
They rubbed the feather on the housefront of the house
         at the center of the town,
and ⟨where they had done so,⟩ the snow disappeared.

When they had gone on doing this awhile,
the snow was so deep it went up past the roofs of the houses.[3]

Later, they say, red elderberries – ripe ones – started
plopping through the smokehole from the beaks
of Steller's jays.[4]

After a time, they went out through the smokehole.
They went to see the Open Beak of Day, they say.

W HEN they had gone along together for a while,   [5.1]
they met a ground squirrel scampering around.   130
The brainless one tore it to shreds,
and he scattered the pieces around.

When they had gone a little further,
they came upon a woman who lived in a large house.
She was wearing a big labret in her lip.

As she was preparing to serve them a meal,
the woman asked them,
«Wasn't my child playing just below?»

«No,» one of them said.
«There was only a ground squirrel playing there.   140
We tore it to pieces and threw them around.»

«Aiiiii! My darling!» she said.
«Door! Shut yourself tight!»
Xhuuuuu. And it did.

Then the one with the best understanding of medicine
turned into ash
and started to waft himself up through the smokehole.

As he slipped out of sight,
«Smokehole! Slide yourself shut!»
  Xhuuuuu. It did so too.   150

He ran to where that one had butchered the ground squirrel.
He reassembled all the pieces
and spat medicine upon them.

The ground squirrel wriggled
and followed him back to the house.
Then the ground squirrel knocked at the door.

«Grandma! It's me!»

«Door! Open wide!
  Smokehole! Slide yourself back!»
When she said so, they did.   160

Then she gave them a meal, they say.
She gave them every sort of lovely food.
That was Rockcliff's house, they say.
She is the ground squirrel's grandmother, they say.

They spent the night in her house.
She fed them again on the following day,
and then they started on their way again, they say.

WHEN they had gone along together for a while,   [5.2]
    they came upon another woman's house.
After she had fed them,   170
they stayed the night in her house too.

When the brainless one saw that the woman lay down,
and saw that she slept,

he went behind the screens, they say,
to where her daughter lay.

He took her sash and tied it on himself.
When he had been in bed with her awhile,
her mother saw them.

She went to the one who looked like a man
and twisted his heart out, they say,   180
and swallowed it whole.
He tied the daughter's sash around the body.
Then he went back to his place and lay down.

When morning came
and she was making them a meal,
she called to her daughter.
She got no reply,
and she went to her.

There lay the corpse.
She started sobbing then, they say.   190
She sang as a deathsong the words
I chopped up my child.
Then they left that place, they say.

W HEN they had gone along together for a while,   [5.3]
    something big stood right in front of them, they say.
They pushed it over,
and it broke the backs of two of them, they say.

There were seven of them left,
and they continued on their way.

W HEN they had gone along together for a while,   200
    they met a little dog   [5.4]
who was lying in the middle of the trail.

One took a running leap across it.
It reached up and bit him in two.

Another took a running leap across it.
The same thing happened once again.
It killed three without leaving its place,
and four were still alive.

W HEN they had gone along together for a while,   [5.5]
they came to the rim of the sky.   210
It opened and closed again and again.

They ran beneath it
and were gone.
Two were caught and cut to bits,
and two were still alive.
Those two did indeed see the Open Beak of Day, they say,

And so it ends.   217

1 Kkyuusta

2 GHADAGHAAXHIWAAS
("White Hillside,"
now *Masset*)

3 Tla'aal (*Tlell*)

4 HLGHAGILDA
(now *Skidegate*)

5 XAYNA ("Sunshine")

6 Qquuna (*Skedans*)

7 Ttanuu

8 Sghan Gwaay (*Ninstints*)

9 Ttsaa'ahl

10 QAYSUN
("Sea Lion Roost")

11 Sheet'ká (*Sitka*)

12 Shaax̱ít.aan
(*Old Wrangell*)

13 Ghasqw (*now Forrester
Island*)

14 *Hlg̱hangaa'u and
His Siblings*

15 Kwinwoq (*Ḵwunwoḵ*)

16 Max̱łaqxaała
(*Old Metlakatla*)

17 Qqaaduu (*Ḵ'aaduu*)

18 Kitqxaała (*Ḵitkatla*)

19 Lhṁdu (*Ḵlemtu*)

20 Wáglísla (*now
Bella Bella*)

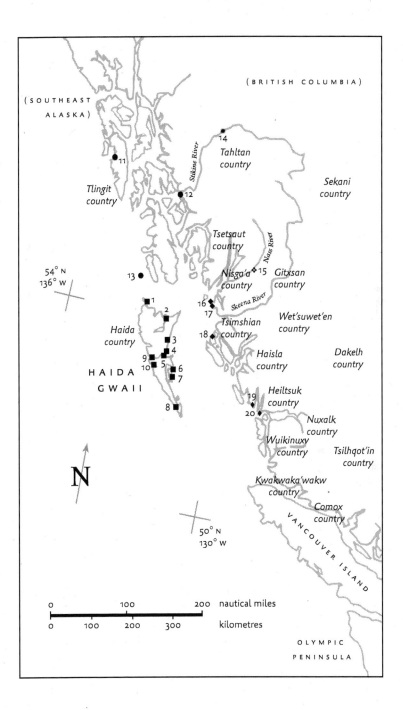

(BRITISH COLUMBIA)

(SOUTHEAST
ALASKA)

Stikine River

14

*Tahltan
country*

*Sekani
country*

11

*Tlingit
country*

12

*Tsetsaut
country*

Nass River

Nisga'a ❖ 15 *Gitxsan
country* *country*

54° N
136° W

13 ●

16 ◆
17

Skeena River

*Wet'suwet'en
country*

*Haida
country*

1

2

3

4

*Tsimshian
country*

18 ◆

*Haisla
country*

*Dakelh
country*

HAIDA
GWAII

9
10 5

6
7

8

19 ◆
20 ◆

*Heiltsuk
country*

N

*Nuxalk
country*

*Wuikinuxv
country*

*Tsilhqot'in
country*

*Kwakwaka'wakw
country*

50° N
130° W

*Comox
country*

VANCOUVER ISLAND

0   100   200   nautical miles

0   100   200   300   kilometres

OLYMPIC
PENINSULA

Appendix 1

Haida as a Written Language

LIKE OTHER LANGUAGES and literatures – including Latin and Greek, Sanskrit and Pali, Chinese and Tibetan, Sumerian and Akkadian, Egyptian and Hebrew and Arabic, German and Portuguese, Italian and Spanish and French – Haida was oral for many generations before a word of it was written. What is unusual is that so much first-class Haida oral literature was patiently dictated and carefully transcribed, and that the identities of the speakers were recorded.

Sometimes, when writing is introduced to a civilization, native speakers are quick to adopt it. Writing and reading spread, and the oral literature shrinks as the written literature grows. A lot of oral poetry may be transcribed (as it was in Greek), or very little (as in Latin). But even when a body of oral literature is transcribed, its survival is not assured. Transcriptions are sometimes heavily edited and expanded or condensed with no attempt to conserve the original record. (This happened early on in Hebrew, for example, and again more recently in Finnish.)

In the last few hundred years, a thousand cultures around the globe have had writing thrust upon them – by missionaries, colonial administrators, or both. This is never a simple event. When writing is forced upon a culture, other transformations and intrusions are always forced upon it as well, and the transition from oral to scribal can't proceed on local terms. Writing becomes a symbol not of language and community, nor of cultural connection to the future and the past, but of cultural dislocation, forced metamorphosis, or foreign domination.

There are generally additional complications. Many communities lack the population or the sedentary habits that make literacy convenient to sustain. Many also have the option (or obligation) of literacy in a second language. In that case, speakers sometimes sense a real advantage – exclusivity or secrecy or adaptability, for instance – in keeping their own first language oral. Many Native American communities – some with substantial numbers of fluent speakers – find themselves in this predicament. So do many speakers of Irish or Scots Gaelic, and of languages such as Romani, Galician, Yiddish, and Kurdish: languages that may attain some regional or local recognition but still have no nation-state or province to call their own. Nevertheless, a written literature offers the present a connection to the past that it would otherwise not have. A flourishing scribal culture also promises the present a connection to the future that it might otherwise be forced to do without.

Many early visitors to the Haida country tried writing a few Haida words and names, but no one, so far as we know, wrote a substantive text in the language until late in the nineteenth century. Beginning in 1876, a series of Anglican missionaries lived at Ghadaghaaxhiwaas (Masset) and devoted themselves to mastering the language – not in order to learn what the most talented and knowledgeable Haida elders could tell them, but in order to preach their own religious faith and promote their own notions of proper behaviour. So far as we know, they were the earliest *writers* in Haida.

The first resident missionary was William Henry Collison, an Irishman, who lived on the Northwest Coast – mostly near the Nass and Skeena rivers – from 1873 until his death in 1922. He was a competent speaker of Tsimshian when he moved to the Haida country in November 1876. Within a year, he could also preach and converse effectively in Haida. Collison returned to the Tsimshian country in 1879 but retained a strong interest in the Haida mission and mentored several of his successors. These included Charles Harrison, who worked at Masset from 1882 to 1890, and John Henry Keen, who was there from 1890 to 1898.

None of the three was a great phonologist, but the conscious analysis and careful description of speech sounds is different from effective mimicry. Their pronunciation may have been far better than their casual orthography suggests. Vocabulary and syntax are another matter. It would be hard to make a case for any one of them as a skillful Haida stylist.

They were missionaries, but all of them were in various ways entranced by the world around them. Collison entered warmly into the lives of the indigenous people he knew. Harrison was more insecure and self-important, less adaptable, less engaged, and less alert. Even so, he was an industrious, if not especially competent, amateur anthropologist. Keen, the least gregarious of the three, was an earnest student of the language and an expert naturalist. But all of them adhered to the priorities of their faith.[1] They saw around them the cultural devastation left by the smallpox epidemics, but they were very nearly blind to the cultural riches: magnificent works of sculpture, weaving, and oral literature, for example. They found nothing worth writing in Haida except their own Sunday sermons and their translations of Christian hymns, prayers, some psalms, and several books of the New Testament.[2] That is why, for students of Haida literature, their work remains essentially irrelevant.

Collison did write English versions of some of the stories he heard in Tsimshian, Nisga'a, and Haida, and it appears that he once imagined putting these versions into a book.[3] Harrison too wrote English summaries of some "quaint old [Haida] legends."[4] But the stories these men heard must have been rendered briefly and off the cuff, not in formal sessions by recognized tradition-bearers and mythtellers. It is not always easy to draw a line between folklore and genuine oral literature, but the distinction is real enough. What Collison and Harrison heard was always on the folklore side of the ledger, or that is how the missionaries perceived it. Haida oratory, which should have been recognizable to all of them as art, made no real impression either.

John Swanton's mentor, Franz Boas, spent most of his life studying the languages of the Northwest Coast and did invaluable work in Kwakwala, Heiltsuk, Tsimshian, Nisga'a, Kathlamet, and six or eight others. With Haida, he did something just as important: he assigned John Swanton to the language and engineered a scheme that would pay Swanton to work full-time on Haida for several years. Boas's *personal* contribution to our knowledge of Haida literature is meagre by comparison: only a few steps up from Collison's. But unlike Collison and Swanton, Boas never set foot on Haida Gwaii. In 1888, at the beginning of his work on the Northwest Coast – when he still saw himself as a geographer and ethnographer more than an ethnolinguist – he located one Haida mythteller in Port Essington, near the mouth of the Skeena River, and three Haida speakers in Victoria. From them, Boas learned a good deal of Haida vocabulary and elementary grammar. He wrote some Haida sentences, but he had not yet grasped the importance of transcribing entire texts. Instead of writing down what the mythtellers said, then working his way through it with their help, he paid an interpreter to translate the stories as they were told. Boas retranslated from English into German, and his unverified German paraphrase, littered with poorly transcribed Haida names, is all that is preserved from those brief and unsatisfactory sessions.[5]

So it is that the study of Haida literature really begins (and nearly ends) with Swanton. He was hardly the first outsider to study the language, nor even the first to do so with pencil in hand. But Swanton was the first person who took extended dictation in Haida, and he took an enormous amount of it, with courtesy, persistence, and intelligence. He took it from those who were best equipped to give it (and paid them, of course, as their tradition and his required). It was not his ambition to tell the Haida what to believe or how to behave. He was there to listen and learn. He was also the first linguist, either amateur or professional, who paid sustained, reflective attention to Haida phonology. He spent a year of his life transcribing the work of every capable Haida oral poet he could find, including Skaay, Ghandl, and Kilxhawgins at Skidegate, and Haayas and Kingagwaaw at Masset. He then went over each transcription with a knowledgeable native speaker of

Haida, weeding out his own mistakes. In addition, he transcribed a number of stories from raconteurs and other non-poets, both good and bad, thereby clarifying many of the differences between genuine oral literature and its imitations and substitutes.

Swanton's transcriptions are not perfect – but no transcriptions are. No orthography or system of notation is perfect either. Nor are there any perfect translations. We do what we can, or we do nothing. By doing what we can, we sometimes make it possible for others to do more. But when our priorities are distorted, we sometimes make it likelier, or inevitable, that others will do less.

Social histories of the Northwest Coast routinely report – correctly enough – that during the late nineteenth and early twentieth centuries, indigenous communities shifted more and more to English. It was the language of the schools to which First Nations children were being sent, and increasingly it was the language of trade and commerce. Where paying jobs were to be had, it was the language of employment. Government agents insisted without fail that it was the language of the future. And since it was the language of the "real" Bible, the "real" hymns – and for Anglicans and Methodists, even the "real" liturgy – why shouldn't it also be the language heard in church? Yet there were clergymen such as Collison and Keen, who had gone to great effort to learn their parishioners' tongue. Where congregations were led by men like that, why shouldn't the church – that bastion of tradition – preserve the ancestral language of the community?

In Native communities at the end of the nineteenth century, the Christian church was not in fact a bastion of tradition. It was, for many, a place of refuge, solace, and support in the midst of population collapse and cultural upheaval, but it was also one of the agents of that upheaval: one of the major causes of the torrent of changes battering Native American life. Many indigenous languages vanished under the onslaught. Those that survived still bear the scars. Some of the changes reached into the fabric of daily speech.

In 1894 – halfway through his eight-year stay in Masset – Rev. Keen's parishioners asked him to stop holding services in Haida and switch to English instead.[6] This has been taken as evidence that, by that date, northern Haida churchgoers wanted to anglicize themselves, consigning their ancestral language to history or to private and inward speech. (John Enrico has referred to a later phase of the same process as linguistic suicide.[7]) Perhaps it really was that simple. Or perhaps it was not so simple after all, as is often the case where the temptation of suicide lurks.

Oral history, mythtelling, potlatch oratory, and Haida singing and dancing did not suddenly stop when Rev. Collison arrived in Ghadaghaaxhiwaas in 1876. Nine years later, the potlatch was outlawed in Canada, but this did not put a sudden end to Haida mythtelling, singing, and oratory either. Eighteen years after Collison's arrival, the monumental works of northern Haida oral literature, like the monumental works of Haida visual art, had indeed largely vanished from public view but not from private memory. In 1894, all but the youngest of Keen's parishioners had seen, heard, and been part of the precolonial Haida world. They had vivid memories of those speeches, songs, and narratives, and the layered richness of the language in which they were composed. The missionaries' translations of the Gospels are – with all respect – linguistically insipid by comparison, and their sermons must have been likewise. Perhaps what some, if not all, of Keen's parishioners really wanted in their church was not *no* Haida but *better* Haida. And if better Haida was beyond the missionary's reach, perhaps good English seemed an acceptable second choice.

Haida translations of the Gospels are bound to be linguistically much plainer than the works of Skaay and Ghandl, Haayas and Kingagwaaw. New Testament Greek is spare, often monotonous, and childlike compared to the Greek of Sophocles, Demosthenes, or Plato. Any translation that suggested otherwise would be dishonest. But Harrison's and Keen's New Testament translations are plainer and more wooden than they need to be. This may reflect the translators' conscious or unconscious assumptions about the intellectual and verbal sophistication of their Haida congregation. It almost certainly reflects the missionaries' own, very unfortunate, lack of exposure to good Haida literary models. But it was the missionaries themselves, after all, who insisted that the old, indigenous ethics and metaphysics were bad, and the new, imported versions were better. No one was going to give them the training they needed in (among other things) Haida poetry and philosophy, and Haida rhetoric and poetics.

Keen, in any case, felt it his duty to persist in using Haida. The causes and effects of that decision are now difficult to assess, but four years later Keen was gone, and the language of church services in Masset has been English ever since.

Keen's and Harrison's New Testament translations, typeset and printed in England as modest pamphlets, were warmly received in Ghadaghaaxhiwaas. That doesn't mean they were widely read. The little books had talismanic value. Some people carried one or another when they travelled; others kept them enshrined in the house. Yet no one, so far as we know, ever clamoured for further instalments, and the books did not, so far as we know, spur anyone to do further writing in Haida.

Swanton was of course not Haida by descent, nor was he fluent in the language. Moreover, he wrote Haida in only the minimal sense: taking dictation from others. He is nevertheless, for now, the one and only Haida writer of any literary importance. His work, with its thorny orthography, was sent to Leiden to be typeset and printed, then published in Washington and New York. Swanton himself sent copies to friends, but the publisher made no attempt to distribute his books in Haida Gwaii. Haida readers were not deliberately excluded, but there was no campaign to include them either. Those texts, nevertheless, have proven indispensable to Haida people who want their language and their literature back. Without Swanton's transcripts, neither they nor anyone else would ever discover, or rediscover, the richness of Haida oral culture.

The "anyone else" part has not been to everyone's liking – but that is how literature works. Literature, oral or written, does what art in general does: it speaks to those who choose to pay attention, and not to those who don't. It is what we call a human universal. This doesn't mean that all humans love or understand it; it means that some humans, many humans, anywhere and everywhere, whatever their own language and culture, can see and appreciate the beauty and the meaning which it embodies. It is not restricted to any social or hereditary or economic group; the only people it can reach are those who are ready and willing to take the trouble to reap the benefits it brings.

In the meantime, orthography marches on. Swanton's way of writing Haida, inherited from Boas, was admirable for its time, but it is needlessly complex, and it leaves a few important things unclear. It was superseded nearly a century ago, and no one has used it for anything since. Beginning in the early 1930s, the International Phonetic Alphabet was updated to include a number of speech sounds found in Native American languages. The American Technical Alphabet – a simpler but equally precise system based directly on Boas's work – also evolved in the early 1930s. These two systems, IPA and ATA, are (like the periodic table and the systems of biological nomenclature) permanently open to further improvement. They remain in widespread daily use as common standards: ATA for any and all indigenous languages of the Americas, and IPA for any and all human languages worldwide.

Over a hundred native North American languages are still in active use, and the most common practice now is not to write them in IPA or ATA only in technical publications. For wider usage, languages tend to develop (or occasionally borrow) their own specific "practical orthography," which is usually some variant of the standard Latin alphabet. There have been several attempts to produce such a system for Haida, and the one that matters most is the one developed by the Haida themselves. This is the SHIP system, created in 2008 by the Skidegate Haida Immersion Program. It is the system used here for all Haida words and textual quotations. A more informal system, as explained below, is used in this book for Haida names where they occur in the translation and in the midst of English text.

A writing system is one thing, however, and spelling is something else. There are very good reasons to simplify and improve Swanton's alphabet, and the SHIP orthography does exactly that. But there is also a good reason to retain Swanton's underlying spelling, rather than bringing it into line with more recent Haida speech. The sounds Swanton wrote are the sounds Swanton heard: as close a record as we can get to the sound of Skaay, Ghandl, and other nineteenth-century Haida mythtellers practising their art. Serious students of Haida literature want to keep Swanton's spelling for the same reason serious students of English keep the spelling (but not the script) of Chaucer, Shakespeare, and Donne. That spelling is information. It is also a reminder that time passes, speech changes, and literacy changes – and that literature persists even so.

Earlier editions of this book (and all editions of the companion volume *A Story as Sharp as a Knife*) use another orthography, not very different from SHIP's, which I adopted in 1999. That earlier system is retained here for Haida proper names where they occur in an English context, not in Haida text. The author of this book, for example, is here called Ghandl of the Qayahl Llaanas instead of G̲andl of the K̲ayahl 'Laanas. I hope this will be understood as a gesture of friendly respect – or at worst a polite convention, like writing Socrates instead of Sōkrátēs and Copernicus instead of Mikołaj Kopernik.

The two systems are shown in full, along with Swanton's orthography and several other alternatives, in the chart on page 187. The essential differences are summarized below. Further details are given in appendix 2, overleaf.

RB (1999)	SHIP (2008)	
gh	g̲	voiced uvular stop
kk	k'	ejective voiceless velar stop
ll	'l	glottalized lateral approximant
q	k̲	pulmonic voiceless uvular stop
qq	k̲'	ejective voiceless uvular stop
tt	t'	ejective voiceless alveolar stop
ttl	tl'	ejective voiceless lateral affricate
tts	ts'	ejective voiceless central affricate
xh	x̲	voiceless uvular fricative

Appendix 2
Spelling and Pronunciation

MANY HAIDA SPEECH SOUNDS are so similar to English sounds that English speakers can hear them and make them with ease. But there are other Haida sounds that have no counterpart in English (or in most other European languages). The Haida letters *a, b, ch, d, g, h, i, j, k, l, m, n, ng, p, s, t, ts, u, y* all represent sounds familiar in English. The other half of the alphabet – *dl, g̲, k', k̲, k̲', 'l, hl, 'm, 'n, t', tl, tl', ts', 'w, x, x̲, ' '* – will need a bit of explaining.

(1) VOWELS: Haida vowels, like Greek and Latin vowels, are short and long. Long vowels are written double (*aa, ii,* etc) and are genuinely *longer in duration* than their short counterparts, not different in the quality of sound.

(2) VELAR FRICATIVE: The velum is the soft palate, toward the rear of the roof of your mouth. Several common speech sounds are made in this location. English *g* (as in *golly*) and *k,* for example, are *voiced* and *voiceless* velar stops. The *ch* in German *Bach* is another velar sound: the *voiceless velar fricative*. In Haida, that sound is written *x.* (A fricative, incidentally, is a continuing turbulent speech sound. Another fricative, common to Haida and English, is written with the letter *s.*)

(3) UVULARS: The uvula is the hindmost part of the roof of the mouth, back of the velum. The *r* of standard French is routinely pronounced in the uvular region; otherwise, uvular sounds are fairly rare in European languages. Standard English has none, but Haida has three, written *g̲, k̲,* and *x̲* (*gh, q, xh*). To make the *k̲* (*q*) sound, start with a series of normal *k*'s (as in *k-k-k-k-kick*)

SIX SYSTEMS OF HAIDA SPELLING

Swanton 1900–1912	IPA 1932f	ATA 1934f	Enrico 1995f	Bringhurst 1999f	SHIP 2008f
a, â, ä	a/a	a/a	a	a	a
A, a̧	ə/ʌ	ə/ʌ	@, a	a/u	a/i
ā, a', ê	aː/aː	a·/a·	aa	aa	aa
b, p	b	b	b	b	b
d	d	d	d	d	d
L., ḷ, l̂, ꓶ	d͡ɬ	λ	dl	dl	dl
g	g	g, g	g	g	g
g·, g̱	ɢ	g, ġ	r	gh	g̱
h	h	h	h	h	h
i	i/ɪ/ɨ	i	i/e	i	i
ii, i'/ei	iː/ei	i·/ei	ii/ee	ii	ii/ee
dj	d͡ʒ	ž	j	j	j
k	k	k	k	k	k
k!	k'	k̓	k'	kk	k'
l	l/ḷ	l/ḷ	l/ll	l	l/ll
l̲	'l/'ḷ	l̓	'l	ll	'l
ł, Ł	ɬ	ɬ	hl	hl	hl
m	m/'m	m/ṁ	m/'m	m	m/'m
n	n	n/ṅ	n/'n	n	n/'n
ñ	ŋ	ŋ	ng	ng	ng
	p	p	p	p	p
q	q	q	q	q	ḵ
q!	q'	q̇	q'	qq	ḵ'
s	s	s	s	s	s
t	t	t	t	t	t
t!	t'	ṫ	t'	tt	t'
L, ḷ	t͡ɬ	λ	tl	tl	tl
L!, ḷ!	t'͡ɬ	λ̓	tl'	ttl	tl'
tc	t͡s/t͡ʃ	c/č	ts	ts	ts/ch
tc!	t͡s'	ċ	ts'	tts	ts'
u, o	u/o	u	u	u	u
ū, u'/ō	uː/ɔː	u·/ɔ·	uu/oo	uu	uu/oo
w, u, o	w/'w	w/ẇ	w/'w	w	w/'w
x., x̣	x	x	c	x	x
x	χ/ħ	x̣/ħ	x	xh/ḥ	x̱
y, i	j/ɥ	y	y	y	y
	ʔ/ʔʰ/ʡ	ʔ/ʔʰ/ʡ	7	'	'
ɛ, '	ʕ̞	ʕ̞	r	[gh], '	[g̱]

Symbols for different but sometimes conflated sounds are separated by slashes. Alternative representations of the same or closely related sounds are separated by commas.

IPA = International Phonetic Alphabet.

ATA = American Technical Alphabet.

SHIP = Skidegate Haida Immersion Program.

Symbols in the penultimate row are all variants of the glottal stop. Those in the bottom row represent the usual northern Haida counterpart of southern Haida g/gh.

and walk the *k*'s farther back in your mouth. When you start to sound like a cawing raven instead of a stuttering speaker of English, you have reached the uvular region. The sound you are making is called a *voiceless uvular stop*.

To make the g̲ (*gh*) sound, do the same with a series of *g*'s (as in *g-g-g-g-gag*): walk it back in your mouth. The end result will be a *voiced* uvular stop. Again, you will sound like a raven.

The x̲ (*xh*) sound is a voiceless uvular *fricative*. To make this sound, start with the velar fricative (*x*), which is the *ch* in German *Bach*, and nudge it back to the uvular region.

(4) GLOTTAL STOP: This is not an unusual sound in human speech, but in English it is an accidental: a sound that plays no formal role and has no letter to represent it. It is the catch in the throat marked here by apostrophes in the interjections '*unh-'unh* and '*uh-'oh*. In Haida too it is written as an apostrophe. In the SHIP orthography, however, *only some* apostrophes are glottal stops. In SHIP spelling, an apostrophe that follows *k, k̲, t, tl* or *ts*, or one that precedes *l, m, n,* or *w,* is really a diacritic, not a letter, and it means the adjacent consonant is ejective or glottalized.

(5) EJECTIVES: Ejective consonants occur in many Native North and South American languages. They're also widely found in the Caucasus and in some parts of Africa but altogether absent from the languages of Europe. Unless you grew up with them, learning to hear and reproduce them will take a little practice.

Most consonants are pulmonic, meaning that they are uttered with airflow from the lungs. Ejectives are not pulmonic; they are made with a sudden burst of air released by the glottis. Your Adam's apple will bounce when you pronounce one. The result may sound (and feel) as though a glottal stop had been superimposed on or combined with the underlying consonant.

Haida has five ejectives: *k', k̲', t', tl', ts'* (*kk, qq, tt, ttl, tts*). Each one of these has to be distinguished from its nonejective counterpart, *k, k̲, t, tl, ts* (*k, q, t, tl, ts*).

If you know a speaker of Haida, Tlingit, Tsimshian, or Nisga'a, Nuuchahnulth or Kwakwala, Chipewyan or Navajo, Lakhota, Keres, Q'anjob'al, or Q'eqchi', Georgian or Chechen, Amharic, Sandawe, or any other language in which ejectives play a role, perhaps you can get lessons face to face. There is no better way to learn. Failing that, audio files and video demonstrations are easy to find on the internet.

(**6**) GLOTTALIZED SONORANTS: Sonorants are consonants with a *smooth* continuous sound, either oral or nasal: *l, m, n, r, w,* for example. Speakers of English sometimes glottalize such sounds. You might, for additional emphasis, begin the exclamation *Well!* with a glottal release: '*Well!* Or you might pronounce the interjection *hmmm* with a glottal release in place of the aspiration: '*mmm...,* or the negative *unh-unh* with no vowels but two glottal releases: '*nnn-'nnn.* In English, these are merely expressive gestures. In Haida, sounds like these play a formal role. The sounds *l, m, n,* and *w* all have glottalized counterparts: '*l,* '*m,* '*n,* '*w.* The first of these, '*l* (*ll*), occurs in Haida third-person pronouns and is therefore very frequent.

Glottalized sonorants are different from ejectives in that the sound *begins* with a glottal release but then continues with air from the lungs. That's why these sounds are written with the apostrophe *before* the letter, not *after* it.

(**7**) LATERALS: English has one lateral consonant, represented by the letter *l.* Haida has six. One of these is spoken and written like English *l.* Another is its glottalized counterpart, '*l* (*ll*). There is also a *voiceless alveolar lateral fricative,* written *hl.* This is a familiar sound in Welsh but rare in other European languages. Nevertheless, it is an easy sound for English speakers to make. Put your tongue in the *l* position and blow air tunelessly out from under both sides of your tongue.

The three remaining Haida laterals are affricates.

(**8**) AFFRICATES: An affricate is a complex consonant that begins as a stop (such as *t* or *d*) and continues as a fricative. English *j* (as in *judge*) – which occurs in Haida also – is an example. A phonetician would analyze this sound as $\widehat{d\mathfrak{z}}$ (= *d* + *zh*). Haida also has a *voiceless alveolar affricate,* written *ts,* and its ejective counterpart *ts'* (*tts*). The three *lateral affricates* are written *dl, tl,* and *tl'* (*ttl*). Here, in each case, *l* represents the sound *hl,* a lateral fricative, not normal *l,* which is a sonorant. Some speakers pronounce the *ts* like *ch* in English cheese, and it can be written *ch.*

(9) NASALS: Haida has the same three nasals as English, written in the same way: *m, n, ng*. In addition, it has two infrequent glottalized nasals, written *'m* and *'n*. In Haida as in English, the *ng* digraph represents a *velar nasal* (as in English *wing*). A mark of separation is included in Haida where the *n* and *g* are distinct, as in the English name *Wingate* or the Haida word *jin·gi* (meaning *next to* or *beside*). The sequence *ng̱* is never a digraph and always means *n* followed by *g̱*.[1]

(10) PHARYNGEALS: The Skidegate dialect of Haida serves here as a benchmark because it is the language spoken by Ghandl and Skaay. There are no pharyngeals in Skidegate dialect, but in Masset and Alaskan Haida, things are different. Skidegate *g̱* (*gh*) becomes a *devoiced pharyngeal approximant* – similar to the *'ayn* of classical Arabic – and *x̱* (*xh*) very often becomes a *voiceless pharyngeal fricative*, like Arabic *ḥa'*. In general, I follow the literary convention that spelling should be consistent across a language even though pronunciation is not, but this approach has limitations. There is one place in this book (p 130) where Ghandl used a specifically northern pronunciation of *g̱*, and I have written the sound there as a turned comma ('). Otherwise, it is written like its southern analogue.

As a general rule, people hear the speech sounds they know but only a fraction of those they don't know. The same is true of meanings: we hear the familiar and miss what is new. For those who are interested in hearing the Haida poets think, paying close attention to both sounds and meanings is worth all the time and effort it requires. To take a very small example: the northern pronunciation of the important name Ghadaghaaxhiwaas is roughly 'Ada'aaḥiwaas. The sounds represented here by the two turned commas and the *ḥ* are sounds that don't routinely occur in any European language other than Maltese. That helps explains why Ghadaghaaxhiwaas was sometimes romanized as Uttewas: some listeners heard the non-European sounds as empty, irrelevant noises, or didn't hear them at all. That's the same kind of error, on a tiny scale, as mistaking a masterful, and highly personal, work of oral literature for a simple anonymous folktale.

Notes to the Text

1 There was never a fixed number of these lineages. John Swanton named and counted 55 in 1900, but a number of these were then extinct as a result of the 19th-century epidemics, and many had divided into subgroups. Including these sublineages, Swanton counted 111 Haida families (58 on one side, 53 on the other). The lists are in Swanton 1905a: 268–76.

2 In the way of supporting material, there is Swanton's grammar (1910), Levine's grammar (1977), Leer's grammar (in Lawrence et al. 1977), and Boas's unpublished Haida dictionary (Boas n.d., wholly based on Swanton's texts). These are all now superseded, for most purposes, by John Enrico's *Haida Syntax* (2003) and his *Haida Dictionary* (2005), and by Jordan Lachler's *Dictionary of Alaskan Haida* (2010).

3 The sole piece of evidence we have for Ghandl's birthdate is his baptismal record (Crosby et al.: 48). This gives his age as 36 on Christmas day of 1887. The church records which might confirm the date of his death (evidently circa 1920) have been missing for many years.

4 These four stories are in Swanton n.d.2: 425–6, 525–6 & 537–9, translated in Swanton 1905b: 292–3 & 325–9.

5 Ghandl's dissertation on the *waahlgal* is in Swanton n.d.2: 630–45, translated in Swanton 1905a: 162–74. Another early Haida example of the same oral literary genre is Kingagwaaw's description of the other major kind of Haida potlatch, known as *sik'a*. This is in Swanton 1908a: 795–800, translated in full in Swanton 1905a: 176–80 and in part in Enrico & Stuart 1996: 8, 11–14.

6 Ghandl's performance of "The Youngsters' Poem" is in Swanton n.d.2: 48–54, re-elicited in Enrico 1995: 68–82, translated in Swanton 1905b:

133–8 and in Enrico 1995: 79–88. See also *A Story as Sharp as a Knife*, chapter 9, and Skaay, *Being in Being*, pp 341–44 (1st ed.) /pp 317–20 (2nd ed.)

7 Gunther 1925: 115.

8 See Curtin 1898 and especially Curtin & Hewitt 1918; Sapir 1909 & 1910 (both of which include material from Curtin); Sapir 1918 & 1921; Jacobs 1929, 1934–7, 1939, 1940, 1959, 1960; Griaule 1948; Turner 1960. Robert Redfield's "Thinker and Intellectual in Primitive Society" (1960) is a useful meditation on the theme. So is Hawthorn's "The Artist in Tribal Society" (1961). Additional examples are published, with Turner, in Casagrande 1960 and, with Redfield, in Diamond 1960.

9 See for instance Reid 1967; Hymes 1981, 1990 & 1995; Curtin & Hewitt 1918.

10 Kwunwoq is Kwinwo'a in Nisga'a, Gunwa in Haida. Harris 1974 – a volume of stories told in English by a Gitxsan chief – is a recent and nonliterary treatment of the Red Feather theme and other mythological motifs. For earlier incarnations, recorded in Haida, Nisga'a and English, see note 1 to the story itself, p 209.

11 Stories confined to historical time constitute a third narrative genre called *gyaahlgalang*.

12 According to Swanton, only one member of this lineage – a middle-aged man named Llaansin (Moses McKay) – was alive in the fall of 1900 (Swanton 1905a: 80, 132; 1905b: 100).

13 Murdock 1936 is a description of Haida potlatch theory and procedure. This description is entirely second-hand, but it is mostly based on memories of procedures followed fifty years before by the Haida poet Kingagwaaw.

14 The term *fractal* was coined by Benoit Mandelbrot in 1975. Mandelbrot 1983 remains a standard introduction to fractal structures.

15 Tenenbaum & McGary 1984: 6. Compare the experience of reading the same texts in this work and its predecessor, Tenenbaum 1976.

16 This is an essential difference between the work of two preeminent students of Native American oral poetry, Dell Hymes (1927–2009) and Dennis Tedlock (1939–2016). Hymes worked primarily with texts that were transcribed instead of acoustically recorded, and his aim was to

expose and represent their inner structure. Tedlock worked primarily with texts that he had taped, and he explored many ways of representing these performances in print. It can be shown that, in a large number of cases, these approaches give nonredundant, complementary results. But for *classical* Native American texts, authentic acoustic analysis is generally impossible, because tapes so seldom exist. Reenactments can be staged, taped and analyzed, but the original performances cannot.

17 John Dunn, in a brief study of Tsimshian poetry, has shown how closely units of thought and units of sound can correspond (and he accordingly describes Tsimshian poetry as metered verse). Tedlock, in his studies of Zuni poetry, shows how much they can diverge – and his descriptions differ accordingly.

18 Holm 1965 is the standard grammar of Haida formline art, but for an alternate approach, see "Components of the Formline" in Reid 2000.

19 *Ars poetica* 359.

20 This shift was marked on the Northwest Coast by the *Arts of the Raven* exhibition (Vancouver Art Gallery, 1967) and by a long-lived and widely travelled show called *The Legacy*, first mounted by the British Columbia Provincial Museum in 1971. Larger institutions in Ottawa, New York and Washington, DC, have, inevitably, changed their course more slowly.

21 Holm & Reid 1975: 202–5.

> THE WAY THE WEATHER CHOSE TO BE BORN >

1 Swanton n.d.4: folios 15–19; 1905b: 21–31; 1908a: 284–92; cf. Enrico 1995: 107–15. The name of the central character, *Sing*, corresponds semantically with Tsimshian *laxa* and Nisga'a *laxha*. It means sky, weather, daylight or air. Another Haida name for the same character is *Sins Sgaanagwaay*, "the Spirit Being of the Air." Toward the end of the 19th century, however, this term acquired new and different connotations, as missionaries borrowed it to preach imported notions of a supreme, celestial deity. Ghandl's poem is now among the best available witnesses to an older Haida tradition. Another fine treatment of the theme, by the northern Haida poet Kingagwaaw, is published in Swanton 1908a: 400–407.

2 A stream and village site on the west coast of Haida Gwaii, not far from Qaysun. The Haida name of this place is Juu, which means rapids or whirlpool or swift water.

3 Octopus is the customary bait for fishing halibut. For a giant halibut, presumably a giant octopus is required. Stories of colossal halibut are widespread on the coast. A good example, told by the northern Haida poet Haayas, is in Swanton 1908a: 575–9. According to the Tlingit myth-teller Léek, a giant halibut created Haida Gwaii, by breaking one original large island up into the present archipelago. (That story, unfortunately, is preserved only in the form of an English summary: Swanton 1909: 180–81.)

4 As a rule, Ghandl structures his works in fives and tens, and narrates them chiefly in threes and fives. The numerology in this story is differ-ent. We begin with ten nephews, but the eleventh man, the slave, is the one to whom the girl finally turns. This "wrong number," in fact, is what sets the story in motion. The boy born from the cockleshell hunts six species of birds – two for food, which he gives to his mother, and four for their skins, which he wants for himself. Next he teaches his adoptive father seven spells for catching halibut. The halibut spells are arranged, however, in a pattern, AABAACA, which is 5 + 2, and when the birdskin capes reappear, only three of them are mentioned.

▸ SPIRIT BEING LIVING IN THE LITTLE FINGER ▸

1 Swanton n.d.2: folios 291–301; cf. Swanton 1905b: 238–47. At Port Essington in 1897, the Haida carver Daxhiigang (Charlie Edenshaw) told a story on the same theme to Franz Boas, but Boas recorded it only in English paraphrase (Swanton 1905b: 247–50). Ghandl's poem can be fruitfully compared, however, with stories told in Haida by Kinga-gwaaw (Swanton 1908a: 417–26) and by Sghiidagits (Swanton n.d.2: 556–61; Swanton 1905b: 336–40; *A Story as Sharp as a Knife*, chapter 5). Other works that invite close comparison are "Ts'ak," told by the Nisga'a mythteller Moses Bell in 1894 (Boas 1902: 117–136); "O'meł," written in Kwakwala by Q'ixitasu' (George Hunt) based on an unnamed oral source (Boas & Hunt 1903–5: 332–49); and "Story of Ganaxnox Sm'oogyit" by the Tsimshian writer Henry Tate (Boas 1912: 146–91). Three Tlingit mythtellers – Deikinaak'w, Kaadashaan and Léek – told related stories to Swanton at Sitka and Wrangell in 1904, but these again survive only in English paraphrase (Swanton 1909: 25–7, 177–80, 215–17).

2 The old Haida town of Ghadaghaaxhiwaas (White Hillside) was trans-formed toward the end of the 19th century into the mission village of Masset.

3 The Seawolf (Haida *Waasgu*) plays a crucial role in Ghandl's story of the Sea Lion Hunter and again in the third trilogy of Skaay's *Qquuna Cycle*.

4 Maghan is a creek north of the old village of Tla'aal (now Tlell), about halfway from Ghadaghaaxhiwaas to Qquuna: sites 2, 3 & 6 on the map, p 175.

5 The beach potato or beach carrot (*Conioselinum pacificum*) is an important wild food on the Northwest Coast. Ghandl calls the plant *hlk'in-xaa sgaawsidaay*, "the forest potato." *Sgaawsit* was apparently an early Haida name for *C. pacificum*, transferred to the domestic potato when the latter was introduced, probably late in the 18th century. After the potato had been integrated into Haida life, its native counterpart came to be distinguished as the forest or wild potato. Ghandl uses the new name, but he expresses (within the myth, at least) a preference for the indigenous, undomesticated food.

   Hlk'inxaa sgaawsit has also been identified as water parsley (*Oenanthe sarmentosa*), but this appears to be a recent extension, if not a plain misapplication, of the Haida term.

6 To "go outside" or "go to the beach" (*kaaxul*) is a euphemism routine in classical Haida. Except in stormy weather, tidewater was the normal place to defecate. A handful of seawater serves very well in lieu of toilet paper and bidet, and tidal action flushes away the feces.

7 These two lines are my interpolation. The syntax of line 285 (see the Haida text on p 24) necessitates a previous mention of the gaffhook. Something – spiritual sabotage, for example – is also required in the story, to explain why the magic arrows fail.

8 It is fairly clear that Ghandl intended a countdown in the number of skeletons contained within the spirit powers vanquished in this tale. These, of course, tell us how many previous suitors reached the same stage. In the alder and the octopus, Ghandl says there were many skeletons. In the sea lion, he says there were three, in the seal two, in the eagle two again. By implication, there should be one set of bones in the clam. I have emended the text to eliminate what I think is an unintended slip.

9 Six rather than ten spirit creatures are mentioned in the narrative, together with two tests (the first and last) that are overcome by shamanic means but that seem in themselves more inquisitorial than shamanic. This makes eight confrontations in all: (1) the burning berries,

(2) man-eating alder, (3) giant octopus, (4) giant sea lion, (5) giant seal, (6) eagle, (7) giant clam, and (8) the big stone basin. But along with the carnivorous spirit tree and five spirit animals, five trick weapons are also mentioned: a gaffhook, two clubs and two digging sticks. One of these (the digging stick linked, very improbably, to the eagle) is pointedly ignored, while the other four are neutralized or destroyed. These four weapons are evidently spirit powers themselves, and with the alder and five animals, they make ten. There are also ten clearly demarcated episodes or scenes in this movement of the story.

10 There is strong evidence that Ghandl "tied the story off" at this point: that he ended a day of dictation, in other words, and resumed on the following morning. The third movement of the story is itself some 350 lines long – typically, for Ghandl, the length of a full story. And there are signs (as suggested in the previous two notes) that, by this point in the story, the teller was suffering some fatigue. Then there is the false conclusion formed by the last two lines of the third movement (lines 470–71), inserted, I suspect, to form a temporary end. I have omitted line 472, which is a verbatim repetition of line 469. I suspect that this line, *Lagan 'l gudangaay 'l giilsgwanangas*, "He took a different view of him," was the first line spoken when the story was resumed. If this is correct, there would have been one other line between 471 and 472 – a line that Swanton says he sometimes heard, but which he always omitted from his transcripts. That line would have said *'La tl siitiiji*, "It is partly finished"; i.e., we are taking an intermission here (cf Swanton 1905b: 270 n 6).

Though I think they are inserted chiefly as a resting point, the last two lines of the third movement are worth close examination:

Ḵ'uuna Kunga nang diinagas g̱iistahaw nawaay 'la tyagang wansuuga
Gyaan 'l ḵuunag̱a, T'iisḵwanaaya, Ḵ'uuna 'lanagaay diitgu staladyang.

The octopus he killed was in the cave at Qquuna Point, they say.
And his wife's father, Rockfacet Cliff, rises behind the village of Qquuna.

Ghandl's Haida listeners would know without having to be told that Ttiisqwanaaya, Rockfacet Cliff, is behind the village of Qquuna. But by saying this outright, Ghandl clarifies a pun implicit in the story. This turns on the words *ḵ'uuna* and *ḵuuna*. The former (with an ejective first consonant) means "edge," and as a proper noun, it is the name of the town near which the whole third movement of the poem takes place. The other word, *ḵuuna* (with a pulmonic first consonant), means "father-in-law."

11 What the canoe eats is _kayuuda,_ wild fruit (usually berries) preserved in oil (usually eulachon). The animal incarnate in the canoe and represented on the hull is therefore probably a bear. Several of the Tlingit mythtellers whom Swanton met in 1904 mentioned a grizzly bear canoe (_xóots yaakw_) as the conveyance used by senior spirit beings.

12 This line has no counterpart in the Haida text, yet a phrase to this effect appears in Swanton's own translation (Swanton 1905b: 244). Perhaps Ghandl said something like this in Haida and Swanton recorded it in his notebook but inadvertently dropped the phrase when typing up the text.

13 Sea otter pelts are usually brown or black, though white facial fur is not uncommon. The rare individuals whose coats are entirely blond or silver are known in Haida as _kuu gaada,_ "white [or bright or light] sea otter," or simply as _giina gaada,_ "white [or bright] creature." The silver colouration develops with age and is not, as Swanton thought, a sign of youth. Skaay mentions a silver otter in _Raven Travelling,_ and silver otters play important roles in other works of Haida and Tsimshian literature. (Examples are cited and quoted in _A Story as Sharp as a Knife,_ chapters 5 & 15.)

14 The killer whales most humans see in Haida waters have one dorsal fin each, like killer whales elsewhere in the world, but in Haida mythology, they frequently have two dorsal fins and sometimes more.

15 Nineteenth-century Haida housepoles often carried three small figures (watchmen) at the top, facing out in three directions. In classical Haida such a pole is _gyaagang kaaji 'laga hlgunuhlsi,_ "a housepole with three heads."

16 Spirit Being Staying in the Cradle is apparently dressed up, for this occasion, to represent his name: his arms are laced to his sides. But there is, of course, a sense in which all killer whales – and all cetaceans generally, when dressed in their sea mammal forms – would fit that description.

17 The central theme of the fifth movement of this story is widely known on the Northwest Coast. In Nisga'a and Tsimshian treatments of this theme, the central figure is usually known as Ganaxnox Sm'oogyit, "spirit-power headman." This name has been borrowed into Haida as Gunanasimgit or Nanasimgit, and into Tlingit as Gamnáatsk'i. These names call the theme to mind, yet plot is generally independent of

persona in classical Northwest Coast mythology, just as theme is independent of instrumentation in classical European music.

► IN HIS FATHER'S VILLAGE, SOMEONE ►
WAS JUST ABOUT TO GO OUT HUNTING BIRDS

1 Swanton n.d.2: 354–8; cf. Swanton 1905b: 264–8 and *A Story as Sharp as a Knife,* chapter 1. Snyder 1979/2007 is a sensitive commentary based on Swanton's translation.

One way of assessing the subtlety of Ghandl's art is, of course, to compare how he and other storytellers deal with shared themes. *K'eła sukdu,* "Mouse Story," by the Tanaina storyteller Peter Kalifornsky (1911–1993) is useful to this end. Neither Ghandl's story nor Kalifornsky's is frivolous. Both address the serious issues of famine and courtesy, and each contains a pivotal scene in which the young male protagonist lifts a mouse over a log that has fallen across the trail. Both stories also, incidentally, link the mouse with fish roe. Because of these connections, among others, these two stories illuminate each other. Yet one is a substantial work of art and the other "just a story."

The clearest point of contact between these stories comes just a few lines after Kalifornsky's tale begins (1999: 138, with corrections):

> Ts'ełt'an quht'ana yeh gheyuł
>   ch'u ch'qidetnik'.
> Heyi niłtu k'usht'a q'u niynik'eset'.

> Yedihdi k'ełaggwa gheni q'ileshteh gheyuł
>   ch'u q'inggwa iditnal'un.
> Yigheni yighetneq
>   ch'u dan'i jenyeghełghel.

> *A man was walking there alone,*
>   *and he was lazy.*
> *He was not giving any thought to winter.*

> *A little mouse was walking through the brush there*
>   *with a little bit of fish roe in its mouth.*
> *He picked it up*
>   *and lifted it over a windfall.*

This too is a story about famine, but there is no marriage, no transformation of birds into women or women into birds, no acquisition and use of medicine objects, no voyage through the mythworld, no ascent to the sky and return to the earth. Only two things happen in Kalifornsky's story: (1) a lazy man is kind to a mouse, and (2) when famine strikes, the mouse repays him with food for himself and his family. Ghandl and Kalifornsky have borrowed from the same stock of widely known themes, but each to his own purposes.

2 The word Swanton uses here is *ts'aa[h]l*, which means pine. In an earlier translation (Bringhurst 1999, p 34), I accordingly translated the term as "pine noodles," i.e., pine cambium, an important native foodstuff for humans but admittedly an odd food with which to tempt a goose. John Enrico has convinced me that what Swanton meant to write, here and later in the story, is *ts'i'aal*. This, as Nancy Turner has confirmed, means the roots of *Potentilla pacifica,* the silverweed or coastal cinquefoil, eaten by humans and geese alike.

3 *Zostera marina,* called *t'anuu* in Haida and eelgrass or seagrass in English, is a submarine plant of the pondweed family, Zosteraceae. People eat the lower parts of the plant – rhizomes, stems and the bases of the leaves. Geese appear to like the upper leaves as well.

4 *Trifolium wormskjoldii,* which grows in tidal meadows, is the common clover in the Haida country and possibly the only indigenous species. The rhizomes are important food for shorebirds, deer and human beings. In Haida the rhizomes are called *naa* and the whole plant is *naahlḵ'aay,* "*naa*-branches."

5 The figure of the one-legged salmon fisherman appears in many works of oral literature from the Northwest Coast of North America and from Siberia. The Tlingit mythtellers Deikinaak'w and Ḵaadashaan link him not to a lovesick husband but to a band of roving brothers – the transformers who appear in Ghandl's story "Hlagwajiina and His Family" (cf Swanton 1909: 22 & 101). A Halkomelem-speaking mythteller known as George Chehalis wove the same figure into a quite different story which he told to Franz Boas in 1890 (paraphrased in Boas 1895: 23–4), and the Kalapuya mythteller John Hudson placed him in yet another context, in a story that he told to Melville Jacobs around 1930 (published in Jacobs 1945: 92–6). For a Yukaghir analogue, see *A Story as Sharp as a Knife,* chapter 2.

▸ THE SEA LION HUNTER ▸

1 Swanton n.d.2: 397–401; cf. Swanton 1905b: 282–5. Swanton gives as the title for this story *Ḵaay kit t'aga nang sta tl' ts'aasdaayagan,* "One they

abandoned because he speared sea lions." The Haida poet Kingagwaaw treated Swanton to another very fine (and very different) meditation on some of the same themes (Swanton 1908a: 385–92). In 1972, two Tlingit speakers, Kéet Yaanaayí and Tseexwáa, dictated related stories to Kéet Yaanaayí's daughter, Nora Dauenhauer (Dauenhauer & Dauenhauer 1987: 108–37).

2 In a normal Haida context, *diigi jaatgalang* would mean "my clanswomen" – i.e., sisters and other women of the speaker's moiety. It could mean the same thing here, if the speakers are brothers and sisters of the slain sea lions. But the social structure of sea lion rookeries is different from that of Haida villages. Sea lion bulls take harems. If only the bulls (the headmen) are speaking – which I think to be the case – the phrase must mean "my wives" instead. There are good reasons, too, why a sea lion bull should ask about his wives and no one else. The bulls are roughly twice the size of grizzlies and are rarely troubled by hunters. Cows and pups are at greater risk. They surround the bulls on the rookeries, are smaller and less aggressive, and their meat is not so tough. Younger male sea lions are at some risk from hunters too, but not so much as cows and pups. And younger males are not the bulls' concern, because they have no place in the social order except as the bulls' replacements-in-waiting.

There are, however, other complications. The people whom the sea lion hunter meets at the bottom of the pool are plainly killer whales. This does not, of course, prevent them from having sea lion forms as well – but why then do they use a sea lion for a cooking box? Moody and Swanton sidestepped this problem by translating *diigi jaatgalang* as "my servants" rather than "my women." This makes interpretation easy but violates the text.

3 The dorsal fins of mature bull killer whales tower over those of the cows and younger males.

4 In other words, she bears the marks of a widow in mourning.

5 Harbour porpoises (*Phocoena phocoena*; Haida sḵul) look a lot like small, misshapen killer whales.

6 There is another pun here. The western hemlock (*Tsuga heterophylla*) and Dall's porpoise (*Phocoenoides dalli*) are both called ḵ'aang in Haida. Dall's porpoises look very much like miniature killer whales. On average, they are also larger and heavier than harbour porpoises – though still no more than a third the length and perhaps a tenth the weight of full-grown killer whales.

7 Ripples along the trailing edge of the dorsal fin are a recognizable sign of age and seniority in bull killer whales. Nicked or notched fins are also seen from time to time. I know of no confirmed sightings of a killer whale with a punctured dorsal fin, but mutilated fins are not uncommon, and these sometimes include white scars that look like perforations from a distance. In any case, the pierced fin, like the doubled fin, is a popular motif in Haida sculpture. Useful sources on the biology and sociology of killer whales include Ford & Ford 1981; Ford, Ellis & Balcomb 1994; and Ford & Ellis 1999.

8 Like chemical elements, the themes in these stories have lives of their own, and they bond with other elements to form new narrative compounds. The Nisga'a statesman Sgansm Sm'oogit, for example, telling stories to Boas in 1894, linked the themes of abandonment among the sea lions, creation of killer whales, and the taking of revenge much as Ghandl did in 1900, but Sgansm incorporates these themes into the story of the hero known as Asihwil or Asdiwal. (His work is preserved only in English paraphrase, Boas 1902: 225–9, and Boas calls him by his English name, Chief Mountain). The Tsimshian writer Henry Tate connects these themes with Asdiwal as well (Boas 1912: 146–91), but for Kéet Yaanaayí and Tseexwáa, these are elements of the story of an ancestor named Naatsilanéi. At Rivers Inlet in 1969, the Wuikinuxv statesman Simon Walkus also told a story about a sea lion hunter abandoned by his brothers-in-law, and he too focused on the taking of revenge – but he linked this theme of revenge against the brother-in-law to another, very widely told, story of a blind hunter's revenge against his faithless wife (Walkus 1982: 100–134). The Tlingit mythteller Kaadashaan ties the creation of killer whales to the idea of revenge against a wife's ungrateful brothers but divorces it from the figure of the hunter abandoned among the sea lions, as well as from the figure of the hunter who dresses himself in the skin of the Seawolf (Swanton 1909: 165–9, 230–31). Kingagwaaw, like Ghandl and Sgansm, links the theme of abandonment among the sea lions to the creation of killer whales, but he insists that the abandonment was unintentional. Revenge has no place in his story (Swanton 1908a: 385–92).

Often, though not always, in such stories it seems clear that killer whales already exist when the carver engenders a new clan of them. So the Tlingit mythteller Deikinaak'w can combine the figure of the expert carver who creates killer whales with the figure of the hunter who must rescue his abducted wife from other killer whales (Swanton 1909: 25–7). And Ghandl's sea lion hunter can meet killer whales beneath the sea before he creates them here at the surface. Perhaps indeed he *must* meet them there, in an underwater dream world, before he can recreate them in this one.

Though it dwells upon revenge, Ghandl's poem ends on a note of praise for brotherhood and loyalty. It is worth comparing the conclusion of Kingagwaaw's poem (Swanton 1908a: 392), where the focus is on brotherhood of a somewhat different order. (In Kingagwaaw's poem, the protagonist's name is Guut·tsa.)

> Wagyaan tlan sihlgaang Guuttsa stiilan.
> Ḵaay kiijaay 'l ḵats'aayan ahluu
> ḵaay gudangaay ga 'l iijinggang.
> 'L gudangaay x̱aadaagang.
> Wagyaan sgaan ising 'l tlawhlaayan.

> *And so, Guut·tsa never went back to his home.*
> *But because he got inside the sea lion's belly,*
> *he remains in the sea lion's mind.*
> *Their minds are human.*
> *And besides that, he created killer whales.*

Kingagwaaw does not, like Ghandl, bring the Seawolf and the hunter who takes its skin into the fabric of this story – but that theme too has a rich existence of its own. It is important to the third and fourth parts of Skaay's *Qquuna Cycle* and is central to another classic of Northwest Coast oral literature: Moses Bell's *Max̱mts'iits'kwł* ("Growing Up Like One Who Has a Grandmother.") Bell dictated the latter work in Nisga'a to Boas at Kincolith in 1894 (Boas 1902: 137–68).

Both the master artist Daxhiigang and the northern Haida raconteur Kihltlaayga link the theme of capturing a monster from the water with the theme of revenge against a mother-in-law pretending to be a shaman (Swanton 1908a: 612–24), but Ghandl is the only classical Haida author who fuses the hunter who traps the Seawolf with the hunter who creates the killer whales.

> ⟩ THE ONE WHO GOT RID OF NINE OF HIS NEPHEWS ⟩

1 Swanton n.d.2: 381–5; cf. Swanton 1905b: 277–80 and *A Story as Sharp as a Knife*, chapter 22. It is well worth comparing this poem with two others told in Haida. One was dictated by Xhyuu (Swanton n.d.2: 371–3, translated in Swanton 1905b: 271–6 and *A Story as Sharp as a Knife*, chapter 20, the other by Kingagwaaw (Swanton 1908a: 513–17). Daxhiigang

dealt with the same theme in a story that he told Franz Boas (recorded only in paraphrase, in Swanton 1905b: 273–6). Another analogue of interest is the story of K'wixalalagilis and Kiłi'lakw, written in Kwakwala by Q'ixitasu' (Boas & Hunt 1903–5: 365–74).

2 The headman of a town is called *'laana awga*, the town mother. Similar terminology is found in a number of cultures throughout the world. Victor Turner, for example, reports a similar practice among the Ndembu (Turner 1967: 22).

3 Spruce bark for roofing (rather than hemlock or pine bark for food or cedar bark for clothing) is apparently what Ghandl has in mind.

4 *Sgunskaxawa* means "all alone." This is the Haida name for the largest size of California mussel, *Mytilus californianus*. The meat makes good eating and the shells make good adze-blades and knives.

5 The three lines in angle brackets are my interpolations.

6 *Skyaal* is the common cockle of the Northwest Coast, *Clinocardium nuttallii*, typically some 15 cm (6 inches) in diameter.

7 The horseclam (*Tresus nuttallii*) is, with the geoduck, far larger and stronger than other bivalves found in Haida waters.

8 This detail confirms what we should now suspect about the uncle. A big topknot (*kyuuyuu jiwaagas*) is the conventional hairstyle for a Haida shaman.

➤ THOSE WHO STAY A LONG WAY OUT TO SEA ➤

1 Swanton 1905b: 36–43; cf. *A Story as Sharp as a Knife*, chapter 18. In 1901, the northern Haida mythteller Haayas dictated another poem on the same theme (Swanton 1908a: 370–76; also in *A Story as Sharp as a Knife*, chapter 18). The story seems complete as it stands, yet it lacks a conventional opening. Ghandl's choice of words in the first line strongly suggests that he told the story as the direct continuation of something else.

2 Big Inlet, otherwise known as Masset Inlet, is the largest sea loch in Haida Gwaii, some forty miles long and up to eight miles broad.

3 The text says *Skyamskun Xiila*, "Pierced by a Blue Falcon." Swanton did not, it seems, ask Ghandl if he might have meant to say *Dats'i Xiila*,

"Pierced by a Wren." A few lines later we will meet another spirit named *Skyamskun T'awjugins*, "Floating Falcon Feather."

4 Again, Ghandl says *Skyamskun X̱iila*, "Pierced by a Blue Falcon," and I have emended his text to read *Dats'i X̱iila*, "Pierced by a Wren."

5 There is nothing in the text to indicate who is the subject in this stanza (lines 186–90). Swanton understood a change of subject, from Ttlaajaat (Fairweather Woman) to Stan Gwaay (the resident spirit of Charcoal Island). I think this reading is based on clarification from Ghandl, so I follow Swanton's lead. Charcoal Island is near Ghandl's birthplace, Qaysun.

▸ HLAGWAJIINA AND HIS FAMILY ▸

1 Swanton n.d.2: 322–33; cf. Swanton 1905b: 252–63. Ghandl gave Swanton two titles for this story: *Hlagwajiina* and *Hlgangaa'u ganga*, "Hlghangaa'u and His Siblings." The name Hlagwajiina is etymologically connected with Tlingit *leiq' k'udas'*, "red rockfish jacket" and altered through analogy with the Tlingit shaman's spirit known as Hlagwa. (The red or yelloweye rockfish – *sg̱an* in Haida – is *Sebastes ruberrimus*, widely known on the Northwest Coast as red snapper.) But there are many more forms of the name, and tracing a straight and simple etymological path among them all now seems impossible. A Tlingit counterpart that Swanton often heard is Lakichanéi. This is probably of Athabaskan origin, related, for example, to Navajo *káá'ts'iní*, "the one with bones on the outside" (now the Navajo term for armadillo). Stories of a child-killer dressed in spiny armour are, in any case, widely told in aboriginal America. Closest to home is one that Haayas dictated to Swanton in Haida in 1901 (Swanton 1908a: 376–82). Ḵaadashaan also told a detailed version of the story to Swanton at Wrangell in 1904, and Deikinaak'w a briefer version at Sitka, but these survive only in the form of English paraphrase (Swanton 1909: 22–5, 99–106). In Tlingit, Swanton transcribed only a tiny scrap of such a story, told at Sitka by Katlian (1909: 297–8).

In 1894, in the Nisga'a village of Kincolith, a Tsetsaut hunter by the name of Dentselé (Levi) told Boas three related stories. Boas transcribed part of one in Tsetsaut (Boas & Goddard 1924: 34–5). For the rest, all we have is an English paraphrase (Boas 1896–7, pt 1: 257–9, 263–4; pt 2: 37–9).

2 Some (and probably all) of these names are corrupted Tlingit and Athabaskan. Hlghangaa'u, for example, appears as Lḵ'ayaak' in the corres-

ponding stories told by Deikinaak'w and Ḵaadashaan, and Jeff Leer has confirmed for me that Tlaaganaaqati appears as Tl'aaḵ'anaagadi in an unpublished story told in Tlingit by Seidayaa (Elizabeth Nyman). The name Hlghangaa'u may be related to Tsetsaut *ɬgaxó,* "copper ring," and Gustalaana to Tsetsaut *'áɬa',* "hand."

3 Apart from the use of Tlingit names, this is the first clue to the setting of the poem. Ghasqw is Forrester Island, a mountainous, wooded and isolated spot some 15 miles off the Dall Island outer shore at the south-eastern tip of Alaska and 40 miles NNW of Qqiis Gwaayaay (Langara Island), the northwesternmost extremity of Haida Gwaii. (Ghasqw is marked as site 13 on the map, p 175.) This was Tlingit territory at least until the 18th century. It is now a wildlife refuge under US jurisdiction. At Masset in 1901, Haayas pronounced the name of the island *Gasḵ'w* and that of the murderous fisherman *Hlaagujinaa.* In his treatment of this theme, the opening sentence is *Gasḵ'w inggw Hlaagujinaa naagan,* "Hlaagujinaa lived on Gasqqw" (Swanton 1908a: 376).

4 *Taadlat Ǧadala,* "Outruns Trout," is a mythname of the swallow, reputedly the fastest of the birds.

5 The *ḵ'iiyaanga* is the lion's mane jellyfish (*Cyanea capillata*), whose redcedar-coloured, poisonous medusae reappear in Haida waters every summer. Like most scyphozoans, they are weak swimmers, rarely out-pacing a freely drifting canoe. Their reputation for speed in the Haida mythworld is based on the number and length of their tentacles. The umbrella or body is often only a metre or so in diameter, yet it supports a thousand tentacles or more. These tentacles, which may be 1–2 m long when retracted, can be rapidly extended to 10 m. In 1865, the marine zoologist Alexander Agassiz reported an individual 7½ ft (2.3 m) in diameter, with tentacles extensible to 120 ft (36.5 m).

According to Solomon Wilson of Skidegate (1887–1979), the Lion's Mane Jellyfish and the Rufous Hummingbird (*Hltants'iigit*) once raced each other to Haida Gwaii from the mainland – a distance of roughly 100 nautical miles. The Hummingbird took the lead at first but kept stopping to rest in mid-air. The Jellyfish drifted until evening, then reached out with his tentacles, grabbed onto the rays of the setting sun and pulled himself across, arriving long before the Hummingbird (cf. Ellis & Wilson 1981: 1).

C. capillata is a circumpolar species. For a thorough description and a review of the technical literature, see Russell 1953–70, vol. 2:

106–26. Arai 1997 is much more up-to-date but deals with this species only *inter alia*.

6 Skookum root – also known as cornlily or Indian hellebore – is *Veratrum viride* (Haida *gwaayk'ya*), an acutely poisonous plant found widely on the Northwest Coast. In traditional medicine, it is used (in minute amounts) as an anaesthetic and purgative. In Haida myth, skookum root and urine are the substances of choice for warding off angry spirit beings.

7 Ghandl has told us (line 307) that the brothers are seeking the head of the child of Juu (Fast Water or Swiftcurrent), a spirit being living near Qaysun (cf. p 31 & p 191 n 2). Kingagwaaw describes the child of Qinggi, another spirit being of the sea, in similar terms (Swanton 1908a: 363):

> *A child was born to Qinggi*
> *And the child came to wear his hair in dreadlocks.*
> *He was not a practising shaman,*
> *and he used to sleep behind his father's house.*
>
> *His feet were on the seafloor.*
> *And nothing but his face broke the surface of the water.*
>
> *And as long as he was sleeping there,*
> *his hair continued floating.*
> *And sculpins flitted about at the tips of his locks.*

The third line of this passage may be spoken tongue in cheek, since it is flatly contradicted by everything else that is said. But according to Skaay, the child of Qinggi – not born but adopted – is in fact the Raven himself.

8 Ghandl calls these creatures *siixas tl't'algaanga*, which means "shrill, argumentative hoverers." Naggers, in other words. The name is used for the pine siskin and more generally, for the whole subfamily of cardueline finches. These are small birds, prone to arrive (especially when migrating over water) in large and noisy flocks. The northern Haida poet Haayas also understands a link between migrating songbirds and the spirit-beings of the sea (Swanton 1908a: 305, where the species mentioned include crossbills and kinglets).

9 *Gyaanhaw xaaydlagwi ising ll gandaxittl'xagaawang wansuuga*: "Then *xaaydla*-ward again he [= they] went-hurriedly-in-a-group is-said-there." They went back toward the *xaaydla*, the boundary between worlds,

which is the intertidal region: a marginal but (for humans) habitable realm. See *A Story as Sharp as a Knife*, pp 120, 155, 331 (1st ed.) / pp 121, 157, 332 (2nd ed.) / pp 111, 149, 328 (1st British ed.).

10 The principal motifs in the third movement of this poem – incest between brother and sister; the killing of a child whose single parent lives in the sea; and the subsequent destruction of the land – are linked in another, very different work from the Northwest Coast: the story of Hak'ulak̲, written in English and Tsimshian by Henry Tate (in Boas 1916: 221–5).

11 Swanton's note to his own translation informs us that the story is not perfectly complete. "One episode, telling how a gigantic mouse was killed, has been omitted" (1905b: 262). No such episode appears in the Haida transcript, nor is there, on the surface, any sign that a passage has been cut, but this explains, I think, why the penultimate episode (§5.4) is so brief and uneventful. The omission was probably made by Ghandl himself, not by Swanton. In fact, the two penultimate episodes, §5.3 and §5.4, were apparently cut short – perhaps because the dictation session had been long and the hour was late.

In the summer of 1901, an unnamed Alaskan Haida mythteller told Moody and Swanton another story about a giant mouse (Swanton 1905a: 258). The story was told in Haida, but Swanton wrote it only in English paraphrase. This is the closest piece of evidence we have from which to guess the shape of Ghandl's missing episode.

12 Around the world there are stories about people turning into rocks. The rocks at issue here are near Telegraph Creek, in the Tahltan country, just below the Grand Canyon of the Stikine River (site 14 on the map, p 175). Stories concerning the rocks are known, in one language or another, to nearly everyone who lives in their vicinity. Ghandl's was the first to be transcribed, though plainly it rests on an old, multilingual, multinational tradition. The only version of Tahltan origin yet published is a summary, given in English only, by James Teit (1909: 318). The earliest Tlingit version recorded is K̲aadashaan's (Swanton 1909: 99f), once again an English paraphrase.

There is another piece of literary evidence concerning cultural relations between the Haida and the Tahltan. Early in the 20th century, an unnamed Tahltan speaker talked to Teit about the difference between coastal and inland indigenous culture. Teit, as usual, despite his skill with languages, recorded these discussions only in English paraphrase. Given all these limitations – no name, no date, no transcribed text – the

record really *is* reduced to folklore. This, however, is what Teit says the
Tahltan speaker said:

> *Raven spent much time on the coast, instructing and teaching arts to the*
> *people there. The coast tribes were particularly his people and children.*
> *Therefore the Coast Indians have greater knowledge in many ways, and*
> *are better provided, than the Tahltan and other Interior Indians. They*
> *have better houses, have boxes, and better tools, than the interior people.*
> *Raven had finished his work on the coast before he came to the interior.*
> *He was tired then, after his years of constant labor, and could not do much*
> *in the interior....*
>
> *Of all countries, Raven spent the largest time in the Haida country. He*
> *took great pains in teaching the people there. Therefore the Haida are more*
> *skillful than any other tribe. They can make all kinds of things better than*
> *the Tlingit and Tsimshian. This is why the Haida are superior to all tribes*
> *in canoe-building, house-building, making of totem-poles, and carving.*
> [Teit 1919–21: 213]

Needless to say, this is one person's testimony, even though the
speaker is unnamed. It should not be misconstrued as "what the Tahltan
believe" – as though all Tahltan thought the same – but it does, like
Ghandl's story, testify to a long tradition of international travel and
cultural exchange.

13 An intriguing passage in §1.1 of Skaay's *Qquuna Cycle* enunciates the
rule "five for the women and ten for the men" (*A Story as Sharp as a
Knife*, p 89 [1st ed.] / p 91 [2nd ed.] / p 85 [1st British ed.]; *Being in Being*,
p 54 [1st ed.] / pp 43–4 [2nd ed.]). Such a rule seems implicit here in
Ghandl's poem as well, where the transformation into rocks constitutes
the tenth death for the brothers and the fifth death for their sister.

All ten siblings are transformed in §1.3.4, when their mother burns
their dog skins. Eight of the nine brothers die their first death in §1.4, at
the hands of Hlagwajiina. Then the sister dies four times at the hands of
her own brothers, in §§2.2–5, and is transformed a second time (§3.1.1)
by menarche. The brothers then die four more deaths (from Fast Water's
fire, §3.2; North Wind's ice, §4.1; through the theft of breath, §4.2; and
again in §4.3, where they knowingly burn themselves up). The fourth
death (§4.2) appears to be a brush with death more than death itself, and
the brothers are saved by Sawahliixha, not revived by Tlaaganaaqati.
The fifth death – a turning point, of course – is the first in which all
brothers are involved and the only death overtly self-inflicted.

Only one (the second youngest) dies the sixth death. His own brothers trap him in his marmot incarnation (§5.1), but all the brothers, by dressing up in marmot skins, pass through a kind of transformation and renew in some degree the quadruped identity they lost near the outset of the poem. This second youngest brother, who does duty for his elders in enduring the sixth death, is the only one who marries and enjoys, albeit briefly, an independent life. Ghandl does not say, but Hlghangaa'u may be this brother's name.

Death number seven, like death number two, seems particularly risky. This is the episode (§5.2) in which Tlaaganaaqati – who nearly dies again himself – at first forgets to resurrect his brothers. The eighth death involves the stone slab and the feathers that are in the care of the Echo spirit (§5.3). The ninth would be the missing episode, involving the giant mouse (§5.4). The tenth, of course, is the final transformation into rocks in the Stikine (§5.5).

Along the way, the brothers seem to kill five monsters and fail to destroy three others. The five destroyed are Hlagwajiina himself, the Lamprey spirit, Put Yourself to Sleep spirit, Echo spirit and (presumably last) the giant mouse that Swanton mentions. The three they fail to destroy are a seagod named Fast Water, the North Wind, and a forest-dwelling cannibal who traps them in his snare. This cannibal is the only monster never named, and it is in his episode (§5.2) that Tlaaganaaqati suffers his lapse of memory. He neglects at first to resurrect his brothers. Perhaps he also just forgets to kill the cannibal.

The abbreviation of the story's last few episodes makes it seem a trifle strange that so much time is expended on the marmots (§5.1) – but marmots play intriguing minor roles in Haida myth. Haayas, for example, tells the story of a shaman whose cane enabled him to cross the Stikine, the Nass and other major rivers. This cane was given to the shaman by a marmot (Swanton 1908a: 590). Perhaps, then, if the brothers had been kinder to the marmots, they might have been successful in crossing the Stikine and made a fundamental change to their own story. I also have a hunch that the one brother's marriage is secretly important to this story. Why this should be so may become a little clearer if the story is read side by side with §4 of Skaay's *Qquuna Cycle*.

Marmots, incidentally, routinely eat the florets of skookum root (*Veratrum viride*), which cause visions, coma or death when consumed by human beings. This may have enhanced their reputation – one which all nonhumans have in some degree – for superhuman power.

➤ THE NAMES OF THEIR GAMBLING STICKS ➤

1 Swanton n.d.2: 519–21; cf. Swanton 1905b: 322–4. Ghandl did not give the story a title. He did, however, tell Swanton that the story belonged to Jaxwi Sqwaahladagaay, "The Ones Who Paddle Seaward," a lineage of the Raven side. As mentioned in the introduction, Ghandl knew a lot about this lineage.

Qay Llanagaay, or Sea Lion Village, was just west of Hlghagilda, at a site now known as Second Beach. It disappeared before Ghandl was born, but was remembered as the mother village of Qaysun, Ghandl's home town, on the other side of the archipelago.

Two other Haida stories about gamblers are worth comparing with this one. They are the story of Sinxhiigangu, told by Tlaajang Quuna (Swanton 1905b: 52–7) and Haayas's story of his namesake, told as the opening movement of his own k'ayaagaang (Swanton 1908a: 756–62).

2 Juujitga or Juuts'itga, "Shooting Rapids," is a waterfall and mountain west of Hlghagilda, where the Jaxwi Sqwaahladagaay were once a leading family.

3 Juujitga names nine sticks. There is necessarily a tenth, which is the trump or ace, known in Haida as jilaay, "the bait." It, however, is un-painted and unnamed, because ideally it is invisible. In daily life, there is no fixed number of gambling sticks in a set. Ghandl's sense of literary form, not historical verisimilitude, makes this set consist of ten. Five or six sticks are sufficient to play the game. Some older sets containing 70 or 80 sticks exist, but these are really multiple sets, from which a player would select a handful, including a trump stick, for any given round.

4 Gambling sticks on the Northwest Coast are often works of art, as chess sets are among Europeans. Serious players may own several sets of sticks, and in former times they carried these around, with other apparatus essential to the game, in a specially made and painted leather bag, often a work of art as well. The sticks themselves are wood or bone, on the order of 12 or 13 cm (5 inches) long, meticulously shaped and highly polished. Each stick but one is carved, painted, branded or inlaid with an individual design, either purely abstract or allusively representational.

The gambling bag typically contains, at minimum, four things: one large or several smaller sets of sticks; a mat or hide which is used as the playing surface; a smaller piece of hide on which the sticks can be displayed; and a quantity of finely shredded redcedar bark. When shredded finely enough, cedarbark begins to fluff like wool. It also yields a quantity of fine dust or powder. Wisps of this bark dust sometimes rise and drift away like smoke as the shredded bark is handled.

Two players sit facing one another, place their bets, and determine who will be the first to work the sticks. This privilege normally goes to the visitor. The stickhandler chooses which of his sticks he will use and displays them, to prove that the trump is there. Then he shuffles the sticks in his hands with enough shredded cedarbark to make them disappear. He drops the sticks and bark down in two piles between himself and his opponent. The opponent must then choose which pile contains the trump. If he fails, the stickhandler scores a point and works the sticks again. If the opponent guesses correctly, he scores a point for himself. Either player needs eight points *more than his opponent* to win the set – but after the seventh point the rules change. For the eighth point, the stickhandler deals four piles rather than two, and the opponent chooses three. The handler has but one chance in four of winning that round – and if he fails to win his eighth point, the score reverts to zero and the set begins again.

5 There is no closing formula in the manuscript, and the coda may have been an afterthought. The quotative used here (translated "they tell me") is the nonreflexive form *wansuugang* rather than *wansuuga*, which Ghandl employs consistently in mythtexts.

> A RED FEATHER >

1 Swanton n.d.2: 542–5; cf. Swanton 1905b: 330–32. Ghandl's full title for this story is *Gunwa 'lanagaay ga t'aagun sgiida ga galsk'asdahlaayagan:* "A red feather lifted up a string of them at Gunwa." Gunwa is the Haida name for the Nisga'a village of Kwunwoq (Kwunwok̲, Kwinwo'a), on the left bank of the Nass, some 40 miles upstream from Kincolith. Kingagwaaw told Swanton a very brief but similar story (Swanton 1908a: 640–44), setting it in Kkun·gyalang, a town on the north coast of Haida Gwaii. At Kincolith in 1894, Moses Bell and Sgansm Sm'oogit dealt at length with the same themes in stories they told to Boas in Nisga'a. Boas transcribed Bell's story as dictated (Boas 1902: 94–101) but preserved only an English summary of Sgansm's (Boas 1902: 234–5). Another work based on the same theme is Henry Tate's story "Nal̲k̲," written for Boas in English and Tsimshian (Boas 1916: 125–31).

Ghandl is the only classical Haida author who mentions *Sinsk'uuda,* the Open Beak of Day. The name is reminiscent of creatures such as

Hoxwhokw and G̱alogwa̱dzo'i, the "Crooked Beak of Heaven," who appear in Kwakwalan oral literature and still play a major role in Kwakwalan ritual theatre. In fact, the whole fifth movement of "The Red Feather" is reminiscent of Kwakwalan oral narrative.

2 The Haida is *jaada indaawang*, "a woman in seclusion," or "a woman to be avoided." This means that she is having her first period.

3 Feathers and snow, linked in the first of these poems, are linked again here in the last. The link attains its meaning through the force of Ghandl's imagination, but its roots are also in his language. Snow in Haida is *t'agaw*; a feather is *t'aagun*. Snowfalls in the Coast Range, straight uphill from Gunwa, are among the highest in the world, but all the Haida and Nisga'a villages are at tidewater. Snowfalls there are light, and snow rarely stays on the ground for more than a week or two.

4 Red elder (the coastal variety of *Sambucus racemosa*) is one of the latest fruits to ripen on the Northwest Coast. It appears that the residents of Gunwa have remained snowed in all summer as well as all winter, yet flowers have bloomed and fruit has ripened everywhere else.

➤ NOTES TO APPENDIX ONE ➤

1 Collison's engaging and informative account of his career (*In the Wake of the War Canoe*, 1915) bears the telling dedication "to the glory of God and the extension of His kingdom everywhere." Collison clearly imagined this kingdom as something so wonderful and pure that its expansion could involve only cultural gain, never cultural loss.

2 Collison, by his own account, translated "hymns and prayers ... portions of Scripture, a catechism, and the commandments" and had prepared "several handbooks" on Haida grammar and vocabulary which he gave or loaned to his successors (Collison 1915: 241). It seems that none of this material was published and almost all of it has perished. There are, however, residual scraps in the Collison fonds at UNBC (Collison n.d.) and in reports that Collison sent to the Church Missionary Society (CMS), as well as occasional tidbits in Collison's published work. A few of the surviving fragments are quoted and closely examined in Tomalin 2011: 75–85.

Harrison published a Haida translation of the Gospel of Matthew (London, 1891) and an anthology, in Haida, of tales from the Old Testament (1893). Keen published translations of the Gospel of John (1893), the Gospel of Luke (1899), the Acts of the Apostles (1898), and selections from the Book of Common Prayer (1899). Both Harrison and Keen also published lengthy sketches of Haida grammar.

3 See mss 2009.7.2.5 & 2009.7.2.8 in Collison n.d.

4 Harrison 1925, chapter 10. The remark about "quaint old legends" comes from a CMS pamphlet, *The Hydah Mission, Queen Charlotte's Islands* (London: Church Missionary House, [1884]), p 19.

Swanton's *Ethnology* and his two volumes of Haida texts and translations had been available for roughly two decades when Harrison published his "comprehensive" study of Haida history and culture (Harrison 1925), but there is no sign that Harrison had even glanced at Swanton's work. Harrison does refer respectfully to Boas (and approvingly misquotes an essay that Boas had published in 1910), yet he shows no awareness of the ethnolinguistic work that had been Boas's chief preoccupation over the previous thirty years.

Harrison's claim to be "a recognized authority on the [Haida] language" (1925: 37) might be accepted as simply a minor exaggeration. Some of his other claims, however, are imaginary or meaningless or both – e.g. (p 43), "Their language contains more words than any other Indian language and also is the most difficult to master."

5 For linguistic information, Boas relied largely on Mrs. Franklin, an otherwise unidentified Haida speaker living in Victoria. The Haida mythtellers he met were George Wiiha from Hlghagilda, Johnny Swan from Qqaadasghu, and an unnamed elder from an unspecified village in Alaska. The German paraphrases of their stories are in Boas 1895: 306–311. For an English version, with helpful notes by Randall Bouchard and Dorothy Kennedy, see Boas 2002: 597–609. Boas's notes on Haida grammar and vocabulary are in Boas 1890, 1891a, & 1891b.

6 Van den Brink 1974: 82, quoting a letter from Keen to the CMS dated 28 May 1894.

7 Enrico 2003: 7.

▸ NOTE TO APPENDIX TWO ▸

1 In my informal spelling, I use the same separator when *t* is followed by *ts* or *tl* (*t·ts*, *t·tl*), to distinguish these sequences from the ejective affricates *tts* (*ts'*) or *ttl* (*tl'*). In the SHIP orthography, this is unnecessary. See for instance the name Guut·tsa (= Guutts'a) on p 202.

Select Bibliography

THE ABBREVIATIONS used here are as follows:

AES = American Ethnological Society (New York)
AMNH = American Museum of Natural History (New York)
ANLC = Alaska Native Language Center (Fairbanks)
APSL = American Philosophical Society Library (Philadelphia)
BAE = Bureau of American Ethnology (Washington, DC)
IJAL = *International Journal of American Linguistics* (Chicago)
JAF = *Journal of American Folklore* (Menasha, Wisconsin, etc.)
NAA = National Anthropological Archives (Suitland, Maryland)
UWPA = University of Washington Publications in Anthropology (Seattle)

Arai, Mary Needler

1997   *A Functional Biology of Scyphozoa*. London: Chapman & Hall.

Boas, Franz

n.d.   Haida-English Dictionary. 4 vols. Holograph. Mss 102.5–102.8, Melville Jacobs Collection, University of Washington Library, Seattle. [Based on Swanton 1905b & 1908a.]

1890   "Linguistics II: Haida," in "First General Report on the Indians of British Columbia." *Report of the British Association for the Advancement of Science* 59: 867–77.

1891a   "Comparative Vocabulary of Eighteen Languages Spoken in British Columbia," in "Second General Report on the Indians of British Columbia." *Report of the British Association for the Advancement of Science* 60: 173–208.

1891b   "Vocabularies of the Tlingit, Haida and Tsimshian Languages." *Proceedings of the American Philosophical Society* 29: 692–715.

1895   *Indianische Sagen von der Nord-Pacifischen Küste Amerikas*. Berlin: Asher.

1896–7 "Traditions of the Ts'ᴇts'ā̈'ut." 2 parts. JAF 9: 257–268; 10: 35–48.

1902 *Tsimshian Texts*. Washington, DC: BAE Bulletin 27. [Actually Nisga'a.]

1911 *Handbook of American Indian Languages*, vol. 1. Washington, DC: BAE Bulletin 40.

1912 *Tsimshian Texts (New Series)*. In one volume with John Swanton, *Haida Songs*. Publications of the AES 3. Leiden: E.J. Brill.

1916 *Tsimshian Mythology*. Washington, DC: BAE Annual Report 31.

2002 *Indian Myths and Legends of the North Pacific Coast*, translated by Dietrich Bertz, edited by Randall Bouchard & Dorothy Kennedy. Vancouver: Talonbooks.

Boas, Franz, & Pliny Earle Goddard

1924 "Ts'ᴇts'aut, an Athapascan Language from Portland Canal, British Columbia." IJAL 3: 1–35.

Boas, Franz, & George Hunt [= Q'iẋitasu']

1903–5 *Kwakiutl Texts*. 3 vols. Jesup North Pacific Expedition 3.1–3. New York: AMNH.

Bringhurst, Robert

1998 *Native American Oral Literatures and the Unity of the Humanities*. The 1998 Garnett Sedgewick Memorial Lecture. Vancouver: University of British Columbia.

1999 *A Story as Sharp as a Knife: The Classical Haida Mythtellers and Their World*. Vancouver/Toronto: Douglas & McIntyre; Lincoln: University of Nebraska Press.

2011 *A Story as Sharp as a Knife: The Classical Haida Mythtellers and Their World*. 2nd ed. Vancouver/Toronto: Douglas & McIntyre. [Reissued, London: The Folio Society, 2015.]

Brink, Jacob H. van den

1974 *The Haida Indians: Cultural Change Mainly Between 1876–1970*. Leiden: Brill.

Calder, James A., & Roy L. Taylor

1968 *Flora of the Queen Charlotte Islands*. 2 vols. Ottawa: Department of Agriculture.

Campbell, R. Wayne, et al.

1990–2001 *The Birds of British Columbia*. 4 vols. Vancouver: UBC Press.

Canada. Department of Fisheries & Oceans
1991   *Sailing Directions: British Columbia Coast,* vol. 2 (North
        Portion). 12th ed. Ottawa: Canadian Hydrographic Service.
Casagrande, Joseph B., ed.
1960   *In the Company of Man: Twenty Portraits by Anthropologists.*
        New York: Harper Bros.
Collison, William Henry
n.d.   Mss series 2009.7.2, W. H. Collison fonds. Northern BC
        Archives & Special Collections, Weller Library, University of
        Northern British Columbia, Prince George.

1915   *In the Wake of the War Canoe.* London: Seeley, Service.
Crosby, Thomas, et al.
n.d.   Church ledger for Skidegate, Gold Harbour and Clue, vol. 1
        [1884–1916]. Unnumbered ms, United Church of Canada,
        British Columbia Conference Archives, Vancouver.
Curtin, Jeremiah
1898   *Creation Myths of Primitive America.* Boston: Little, Brown.
Curtin, Jeremiah, & J.N.B. Hewitt
1918   *Seneca Fiction, Legends, and Myths.* Washington, DC: BAE
        Annual Report 32.
Dauenhauer, Nora Marks, & Richard Dauenhauer
1987   *Haa Shuká, Our Ancestors: Tlingit Oral Narratives.* Seattle:
        University of Washington Press.
Diamond, Stanley, ed.
1960   *Culture in History: Essays in Honor of Paul Radin.* New York:
        Columbia University Press.
Douglas, George W., Gerald B. Stanley & Del Meidinger, ed.
1989–94 *The Vascular Plants of British Columbia.* 4 vols. Victoria, BC:
         Ministry of Forests.
Duff, Wilson, & Michael Kew
1958   "Anthony Island, A Home of the Haidas." Victoria: *Provincial
        Museum of Natural History and Anthropology Report for the
        Year 1957:* C37–C64.
Dunn, John A.
1989   "Tsimshian Poetics." In *General and Amerindian Linguistics: In
        Remembrance of Stanley Newman,* edited by Mary Ritchie Key
        & Henry M. Hoenigswald. Berlin: Mouton de Gruyter: 395–
        406.

Durlach, Theresa Mayer

1928   *The Relationship Systems of the Tlingit, Haida and Tsimshian.*
New York: Publications of the AES 11.

Ellis, David W., & Solomon Wilson

1981   *The Knowledge and Usage of Marine Invertebrates by the
Skidegate Haida People of the Queen Charlotte Islands.*
[Skidegate, BC]: Queen Charlotte Islands Museum Society.

Enrico, John, ed.

1995   *Skidegate Haida Myths and Histories.* Skidegate, BC: Queen
Charlotte Islands Museum Press.

2003   *Haida Syntax.* 2 vols. Lincoln: University of Nebraska Press.

2005   *Haida Dictionary.* 2 vols. Fairbanks: Alaska Native Language
Center / Juneau: Sealaska Heritage Institute.

Enrico, John, & Wendy Bross Stuart

1996   *Northern Haida Songs.* Lincoln: University of Nebraska Press.

Ford, John K.B., & Graeme M. Ellis

1999   *Transients: Mammal-Hunting Killer Whales of British
Columbia, Washington, and Southeastern Alaska.* Vancouver:
UBC Press.

Ford, John K.B.; Graeme M. Ellis; Kenneth C. Balcomb

1994   *Killer Whales: The Natural History and Genealogy of Orcinus
orca in British Columbia and Washington State.* Vancouver:
UBC Press.

Ford, John K.B., & Deborah Ford

1981   "The Killer Whales of B.C." Vancouver: *Waters* 5.1 (special
issue).

Gottesfeld, Leslie Johnson

1992   "The Importance of Bark Products in the Aboriginal
Economies of Northwestern British Columbia." New York:
Economic Botany 46.2: 145–157.

Griaule, Marcel

1948   *Dieu d'eau: Entretiens avec Ogotemmêli.* Paris: Chène.

1965   *Conversations with Ogotemmêli: An Introduction to Dogon
Religious Ideas.* Oxford: Oxford University Press. [Translation
of Griaule 1948.]

Gunther, Erna

1925   *Klallam Tales.* Seattle: UWPA 1.4: 113–170.

Harris, Kenneth B.

1974   *Visitors Who Never Left: The Origin of the People of
Damelahamid.* Vancouver: UBC Press.

Harrison, Charles

1895   "Haida Grammar," edited by Alexander F. Chamberlain.
        Transactions of the Royal Society of Canada, 2nd series, vol. 1,
        §II, part VII: 123–226

1925   *Ancient Warriors of the North Pacific.* London: Weatherby.

Hawthorn, Harry B.

1961   "The Artist in Tribal Society: The Northwest Coast." In *The
        Artist in Tribal Society,* edited by Marian W. Smith. London:
        Routledge & Kegan Paul: 59–70.

Holm, Bill

1965   *Northwest Coast Indian Art: An Analysis of Form.* Seattle:
        University of Washington Press.

Holm, Bill, & Bill Reid

1975   *Form and Freedom: A Dialogue on Northwest Coast Indian Art.*
        Houston: Institute for the Arts, Rice University. [Reissued as
        *Indian Art of the Northwest Coast: A Dialogue on
        Craftsmanship and Aesthetics.* Vancouver/Toronto: Douglas
        & McIntyre, 1978.]

Hymes, Dell

1981   *"In Vain I Tried to Tell You": Essays in Native American
        Ethnopoetics.* Philadelphia: University of Pennsylvania Press.

1990   "Mythology." In *Handbook of North American Indians,* vol. 7:
        Northwest Coast. Washington, DC: Smithsonian Institution:
        593–601.

1995   "Na-Dene Ethnopoetics, A Preliminary Report: Haida and
        Tlingit." In *Language and Culture in Native North America,*
        edited by Michael Dürr, Egon Renner & Wolfgang
        Oleschinski. Munich: Lincom: 265–311.

2003   *Now I Only Know So Far: Essays in Ethnopoetics.* Lincoln:
        University of Nebraska Press.

Jacobs, Melville

1929   *Northwest Sahaptin Texts,* 1. Seattle: UWPA 2.6.

1934–7 *Northwest Sahaptin Texts.* 2 vols. New York: Columbia
        University Contributions to Anthropology 19.1–2.

1939   *Coos Narrative and Ethnologic Texts.* Seattle: UWPA 8.1.

1940   *Coos Myth Texts.* Seattle: UWPA 8.2.

1945   *Kalapuya Texts.* 3 parts. Seattle: UWPA 11.1–3.

1959   *The Content and Style of an Oral Literature.* Chicago:
        University of Chicago Press.

1960   *The People Are Coming Soon: Analyses of Clackamas Chinook Myths and Tales.* Seattle: University of Washington Press.

Kalifornsky, Peter

1974   *K'eła Sukdu,* transcribed by James Kari. Fairbanks: ANLC.

1986   "Mouse Story." Anchorage: *Alaska Quarterly Review* 4.3–4: 173–174. [Translation of Kalifornsky 1974.]

1999   "K'eła Sukdu / The Mouse Story." In *Alaska Native Writers, Storytellers and Orators,* edited by Ronald Spatz et al. Anchorage: Alaska Quarterly Review Press: 138–142. [Revised from Kalifornsky 1974 & 1986.]

Kane, Sean

1998   *Wisdom of the Mythtellers.* 2nd ed. Peterborough, Ontario: Broadview.

Keen, John Henry

1906   *A Grammar of the Haida Language.* London: Society for Promoting Christian Knowledge.

Kuhnlein, Harriet V., & Nancy J. Turner

1991   *Traditional Plant Foods of Canadian Indigenous Peoples.* New York: Gordon & Breach.

Lachler, Jordan

2010   *Dictionary of Alaskan Haida.* Juneau: Sealaska Heritage Institute.

Lawrence, Erma, et al.

1977   *Haida Dictionary,* edited by Jeff Leer. Fairbanks: ANLC.

Levine, Robert D.

1977   The Skidegate Dialect of Haida. Ph.D. dissertation, Columbia University, New York.

MacDonald, George F.

1983   *Haida Monumental Art.* Vancouver: UBC Press.

Mandelbrot, Benoit B.

1975   *Les Objets fractals: forme, hasard et dimension.* Paris: Flammarion.

1983   *The Fractal Geometry of Nature.* 2nd ed. New York: W. H. Freeman.

Murdock, George P.

1936   *Rank and Potlatch among the Haida.* Yale University Publications in Anthropology 13. New Haven, Conn.: Yale University Press.

Redfield, Robert

1960   "Thinker and Intellectual in Primitive Society." In Diamond: 3–18.

Reid, Bill

1967 "The Art: An Appreciation," in *Arts of the Raven: Masterworks by the Northwest Coast Indian,* by Wilson Duff et al. Vancouver: Vancouver Art Gallery. [Reprinted in Reid 2000.]

2009 *Solitary Raven: The Essential Writings,* edited by Robert Bringhurst. 2nd ed. Vancouver/Toronto: Douglas & McIntyre.

Russell, Frederick Stratten

1953–70 *The Medusae of the British Isles.* 2 vols. Cambridge: Cambridge University Press.

Sapir, Edward

1909 *Wishram Texts.* Publications of the AES 2. Leiden: E.J. Brill. [Reprinted in *Collected Works,* vol. 7 (1990).]

1910 *Yana Texts.* Berkeley: University of California Publications in American Archaeology and Ethnology 9.1: 1–235.

1918 "Tom." Ottawa: *Canadian Courier* 7 [Reprinted, with cuts restored, in *Collected Works,* vol. 4 (1994): 450–456.]

1921 "The Life of a Nootka Indian." Kingston, Ontario: *Queen's Quarterly* 28: 232–243, 351–367. [Reprinted as "Sayach'apis, a Nootka Trader" in *Collected Works,* vol. 4 (1994): 481–506.]

1989– *Collected Works.* 16 vols. Berlin: Mouton de Gruyter.

Scudder, Geoffrey G.E., & Nicholas Gessler

1989 *The Outer Shores.* Skidegate, BC: Queen Charlotte Islands Museum.

Snyder, Gary

1976 "The Politics of Ethnopoetics." Boston: *Alcheringa* n.s. 2.2: 13–22.

1979 *He Who Hunted Birds in His Father's Village: The Dimensions of a Haida Myth.* Bolinas, California: Grey Fox.

2007 *He Who Hunted Birds in His Father's Village: The Dimensions of a Haida Myth.* 2nd ed., with a foreword by Robert Bringhurst. [Berkeley]: Shoemaker Hoard.

Skaay of the Qquuna Qiighawaay

2001 *Being in Being: The Collected Works of a Master Haida Mythteller,* edited & translated by Robert Bringhurst. Vancouver: Douglas & McIntyre. [2nd ed., Madeira Park, BC: Douglas & McIntyre, 2023]

Swanton, John R.

n.d.1 Haida notebooks. 2 vols. Holograph. Ms 4162, NAA.

n.d.2 Skidegate Haida texts. Typescript with holograph corrections. ACLS ms N1.5 = Freeman 1543, APSL, Philadelphia.

n.d.3   Skidegate Haida texts. Ms 7047, NAA. [Uncorrected carbon of an earlier state of Swanton n.d.2.]

n.d.4   Masset Haida texts. Typescript with holograph corrections. ACLS ms N1.4 = Freeman 1544, APSL, Philadelphia.

1905a   *Contributions to the Ethnology of the Haida.* Jesup North Pacific Expedition 5.1. New York: AMNH.

1905b   *Haida Texts and Myths: Skidegate Dialect.* Washington, DC: BAE Bulletin 29.

1908a   *Haida Texts: Masset Dialect.* Jesup North Pacific Expedition 10.2. New York: AMNH.

1908b   "Social Conditions, Beliefs and Linguistic Relationships of the Tlingit Indians." Washington, DC: BAE Annual Report 26: 391–486.

1909   *Tlingit Myths and Texts.* Washington, DC: BAE Bulletin 39.

1910   *Haida: An Illustrative Sketch.* Washington, DC: Government Printing Office. [Reissued in Boas 1911: 205–282.]

Tedlock, Dennis

1983   *The Spoken Word and the Work of Interpretation.* Philadelphia: University of Pennsylvania Press.

1999   *Finding the Center: The Art of the Zuni Storyteller.* 2nd ed. Lincoln: University of Nebraska Press.

Teit, James

1909   "Two Tahltan Traditions." JAF 22: 314–318.

1919–21 "Tahltan Tales." 3 parts. JAF 32: 198–250; 34: 223–253, 335–356.

Tenenbaum, Joan M., ed.

1976   *Dena'ina Sukdu'a: Tanaina Stories.* 4 vols. Fairbanks: ANLC. [Revised as Tenenbaum & McGary 1984.]

Tenenbaum, Joan M., & Mary Jane McGary, ed.

1984   *Dena'ina Sukdu'a: Traditional Stories of the Tanaina Athabaskans.* Fairbanks: ANLC. [Revised from Tenenbaum 1976.]

Tomalin, Marcus

2011   *"And he knew our language": Missionary Linguistics on the Pacific Northwest Coast.* Amsterdam & Philadelphia: John Benjamins.

Turner, Nancy Jean

1974   *Plant Taxonomic Systems and Ethnobotany of Three Contemporary Indian Groups of the Pacific Northwest.* Victoria, BC: *Syesis* 7, Supplement 1.

1979   *Plants in British Columbia Indian Technology.* Victoria, BC: British Columbia Provincial Museum.

1995   *Food Plants of Coastal First Peoples.* 2nd ed. Vancouver: UBC Press.

2004   *Plants of Haida Gwaii.* Winlaw, BC: Sono Nis.

Turner, Victor W.

1960   "Muchona the Hornet, Interpreter of Religion." In Casagrande: 333–355. [Reprinted as chapter 6 in Turner 1967.]

1967   *The Forest of Symbols: Aspects of Ndembu Ritual.* Ithaca, NY: Cornell University Press.

Walkus, Simon

1982   *Oowekeeno Oral Traditions as Told by the Late Chief Simon Walkus Sr.,* edited by Susanne Storie & John C. Rath. Mercury Series 84. Ottawa: National Museums of Canada.